About Emily Writes

Emily Writes is a mother of two, a popular author, and editor of The Spinoff Parents. Her first book *Rants in the Dark: From One Tired Mama to Another* was published by Penguin Random House in March 2017. Emily is an advocate for mothers and children, and a volunteer and ambassador for charities supporting parents and families. She lives in Wellington with her very lovely husband and her three-year-old and five-year-old babies Ronnie and Eddie.

Emily Writes
and friends

Is it bedtime yet?

*Parenting ... the hilarious,
the hair-raising, the heart-breaking*

RANDOM HOUSE
NEW ZEALAND

RANDOM HOUSE

UK | USA | Canada | Ireland | Australia
India | New Zealand | South Africa | China

Random House is an imprint of the Penguin Random House group of companies, whose addresses can be found at global.penguinrandomhouse.com.

Penguin
Random House
New Zealand

First published by Penguin Random House New Zealand, 2018

1 3 5 7 9 10 8 6 4 2

This collection © Penguin Random House New Zealand, 2018
© in individual stories remains with the authors

The moral right of the authors has been asserted.

All rights reserved. Without limiting the rights under copyright reserved above, no part of this publication may be reproduced, stored in or introduced into a retrieval system, or transmitted, in any form or by any means (electronic, mechanical, photocopying, recording or otherwise), without the prior written permission of both the copyright owner and the above publisher of this book.

Design and illustrations by Rachel Clark © Penguin Random House New Zealand
Author photograph by Chris Tse
Prepress by Image Centre Group
Printed and bound in Australia by Griffin Press,
an Accredited ISO AS/NZS 14001 Environmental Management Systems Printer

A catalogue record for this book is available from the National Library of New Zealand.

ISBN 978-0-14-377283-5
eISBN 978-0-14-377284-2

penguin.co.nz

MIX
Paper from
responsible sources
FSC FSC™ C009448
www.fsc.org

For Abel, Adeline, Alice, Arthur, Augustine, Aurelia, Ben, Bobbie, Charlie, Corin, Cormac, Davy, Digby, Eddie, Eli, Elias, Emmy, Esther, Evelyn, Florence, Fredrika, Hazel, Henry, Iriphāpeti, Isaac, James, Kaahuia, Kowhai, Liam, Luca, Magnus, Margaret, Mason, Ngaire, Nina, Oscar, Otto, Rebecca, Ronnie, Scarlett, Tessie, Tommy and Vann

Not a day goes by that we don't think about how lucky we are to have you. You have transformed our worlds and we couldn't love you more. Thank you for being you.

Contents

For You 11

Welcome to the world, Mama 15

An essential list of essential essentials for your new baby 19

The legend of the Relaxed Mother 23

Translating the crap we say at
coffee group about our kids 27

Babies and time: The stolen and beloved minutes,
weeks, days, nights and years 32

The story of a mum (who tried her best
but needed a rest) 39

Biological roulette: Coping after birth goes seriously wrong 44

Dispatches from a long night featuring vomit 50

Top tips for getting your baby to sleep 55

Four 58

Just one thing: How to calm yourself when
parenting is too hard 62

Surviving daylight saving when you have kids 66

Rock-a-bye my balls: Why having a vasectomy
made me truly appreciate The Wiggles 70

Magic moments 74

The science of motherhood 78

The rules of birthday parties for children 82

I'm not babysitting and mums are getting
a raw deal: A dad on gender roles in parenting 90

'Are you Nana?' and other tales of older motherhood 94

A parenting glossary 101

Pull your weight: If there's two of you,
you both need to parent 104

My baby slept through the night six times so now
I'm an expert on getting your kid to do that 111

Will I remember this? 117

Screen time isn't the enemy 119

Surviving Wine Mum Night 122

Duking it out with my partner over whose life is harder 126

Terrible and great crowdsourced hacks to make
you feel better about your adequate parenting 131

I'm sorry I white-washed your world:
A letter to my Māori daughter 135

How to survive the school holidays 140

The Masterbatorium: A queer experience of conceiving 147

Parenting confessions 151

How to successfully take a shit after giving birth 156

Same DNA, same brain, same sleep patterns — right?
What being a twin mum has taught me about child sleep 160

Staring at the night sky: Reaching a
diagnosis and saving our daughter 165

Six key benefits of extreme sleep deprivation
inflicted by a tiny human or tiny humans 170

A recording was made of a mother one morning,
beginning at 5 a.m. 174

Stay-at-home dadding — the reality 178

Defending being defensive about co-sleeping 184

Fearless at five 190

When you're tired enough:
On the hell of having a child who just won't sleep 193

The word I wish I could take back 199

10 parenting styles that are definitely
a thing and aren't made up 203

'Today, I'm going back on my antidepressants':
A stay-at-home mum on tackling depression 209

Are mum groups on Facebook a vortex to hell? 213

My babies don't move: A story of physio,
growth charts and slow walkers 218

How to survive severe sleep deprivation —
by someone who is living it 222

Meats, shoots and leaves — A mum finds
peace with what her child eats 229

'I didn't know who was failing — me or him':
On having a child who can't read 233

No Holiday: On the decision
whether to have 'another' 238

A whole good day: When parenting
finally feels like you thought it would 243

My son is turning five tomorrow 247

Acknowledgements 251

For You

Over the past three years, I have spoken to many mothers. Mostly online, some in desperate late-night phone calls, others in person over coffee as we bounced babies on our knees or chased toddlers around the park. I have talked to them at the school gate, at the supermarket, in the hallways at hospitals and in cafés across the country.

Many of these conversations have been tear-filled. Some have been permeated by desperate sobs. Many mothers today are hurting. And they're hurting because of isolation and a dominant narrative that is telling them they're alone and they're making the wrong choices as parents.

We need a village. And we need to support each other to understand that while parenting is a shared experience, we all have differing experiences — and that is OK.

Our different stories don't divide us, they can unite us. And, more importantly, they can help us all in so many ways. They can help us be better mothers to *all* children, not just our own. And they can help us be kinder and more patient with other mothers, too. Understanding helps us all. When you understand why another mother feels the way she does it's almost impossible to feel distant from her.

We teach our children empathy and kindness. We need to

do the same for ourselves and each other. We need to reach out where we can and share our stories so we have common ground.

We are so time-poor and so busy caring for others that it's hard to find the time to care for ourselves. And our well of empathy can be dry at the end of the day, after it has been sapped by our loved ones. It can be challenging to extend that empathy to others — I struggle with it and I know at times I've really failed in the past.

But what helps me to rise above pettiness and nastiness and reject a single harmful narrative about what it means to be a good mother is to speak to other mothers and hear their stories.

I've heard from the mums who are crying in the car park after dropping off their child at 7 a.m., and it has made me admonish myself for the judgements I might have made in the past, based on my own privilege.

I've heard from the mums who have struggled to parent completely on their own or with a partner who is no longer living with them, and it's made me recognise that I can't ever know what that's like.

I've heard from mums who have talked about the emotional pain of seeing their child feel physical pain from sensory issues, and it's made me realise how little we support children who aren't neurotypical.

I've heard from mothers recovering from abuse who have had to make choices that prioritise their mental health so they can be the best mothers they can be, and I've been shocked by my inability to previously view their choices through that lens.

There is not ever a time that listening to others doesn't help us. Every story we listen to, every attempt at understanding, every hand that reaches across the divide helps us.

We make each other human.

We must challenge the idea that we should not share. We must reject the notion that motherhood isn't important. That mothers are not worthy.

Motherhood may be ordinary, but it is extraordinary too.

We are ordinary *and* extraordinary mothers, and we need each other. We need to help each other to get through, and we especially need to help the mothers who are feeling lost and alone.

And that's how this book was born.

The Spinoff Parents was the original home of many of these stories. With the generous support of Flick Electric and The Spinoff team, I've been able to source stories from all over New Zealand from parents with vastly different experiences and circumstances. Together, with the incredible readership we are privileged to have, a beautiful online village for parents has been created. Mothers, fathers, grandparents, aunties, uncles, and would-be, want-to-be, wish-they-were parents have come together to support each other and share with each other.

These stories, born from this space, will make you laugh till you wheeze, make you cry and feel seen. At least, that's what I hope.

The brilliant and amazing writer Chimamanda Ngozi Adichie has talked about the danger of a single story. I see that so much in today's media — traditional or social. I see so little complexity and so much focus on one choice, without any understanding that mothers today do not all have the same choices.

When that single narrative was smashed by these stories and these mothers — what emerged was a beautiful tapestry of experience — I felt free. It gave me permission to fail, to be better, to give up on perfection and instead embrace joy.

Then I began to wonder how we could ensure all parents and parents-to-be could hear from each other. How maybe, finally, there could be a book of these voices, without advice, judgement or rules.

Could we build our village through a book? Each page a brick? Could we create something that parents can return to time and time again — to feel lifted, to feel solidarity, to feel hope?

It is my hope that this book will make you laugh, will bring you comfort, will empower you as a parent. It is my hope that it will be your companion, will walk with you on this path so many have walked before.

Each voice is different, for our journeys are not always alike — but there are shared truths. We know that all-encompassing love, and we know that sense of isolation that can seep in.

I want this book to be your non-judgemental coffee group. Your hidden chocolate. Your glass of bubbles with a strawberry in it. I hope as you read it you think 'Thank God', 'Finally', 'Yes!', and more.

A friend in the night. A reminder that you're seen.

Arohanui
Your friend
Emily

Welcome to the world, Mama

BY EMILY WRITES

When a baby is born, we say welcome. Here is this world for you, precious baby. Here are the people who love you, who will always try to keep you safe. Here are the ones who will care for you, and hold you in their arms and in their hearts.

Here is the world we made for you. It's small at first, four walls and tiny bassinet, a blanket handed down or made with love or bought for $2.99. Here is your home.

And they sleep and cry and feed, and you watch and watch and watch — wanting to hold every second of this time. To feel it all. Your heart is on the outside now and it's beautiful and painful and raw and incredible.

And we say welcome, baby, welcome to this world. We will try to make it better for you. We will try to make it so that when you leave your little room, it's a beautiful world for you.

And we focus on baby, because of course we do. They're new. They're here, finally.

But someone else is new too.

Welcome, Mama.

You wanted this for so long — maybe it was so hard to get here, but now you're here. Maybe it wasn't, or you didn't expect it, and now you're here.

You're here. Welcome.

Welcome to this new world that makes your head spin with love and hope and fear and confusion.

Welcome. The days will be long and the years short. You'll feel alone sometimes, but you're not. You'll feel isolated and it will take time to find your groove. But you're surrounded by love, I promise.

There's a village out there waiting for you. You're part of something. Those of us who have been there want to celebrate this with you and say welcome. Welcome to this wonderful place — we're glad you're here. No matter what your journey, your story is shared.

Somewhere is a mama just like you — who feels those same fears, that same crushing joy, that same anxiety and hope and that feeling of 'How do I do this?' She's out there looking out the window too, cradling a tiny baby and rocking side to side.

She's out there in the room next to you in the children's ward, head pressed against the red cot bars, praying to a god or science or nobody or all of the above, 'please, please, please'.

She's out there quietly nursing a cold coffee at the mums' group she was so scared to go to because meeting new people makes her nervous, and she wants to join in the conversation but everyone seems so confident.

She needs to find you. You need to find her.

And then your days will be filled with tears of laughter and tears of frustration, together. Coffee and cake and a patchwork blanket on the floor. Helping each other latch or make up a bottle. Asking about sleep and solids and tummy time. You'll love her child as dearly as you love yours. Your group of mums will grow and your days will be bathed in a soft light. The sun will fill the lounge as you giggle over your babies lying next to each other on baby blankets. You'll share wipes and nappies and tea and fears and frustrations and truths you never thought you'd say out loud.

You'll feel strong with them and you'll reach for them when you don't feel strong. Please reach for them.

Welcome to this world. You're going to find your people. They're going to help you and you're going to help them.

We're glad you're here. Your light will come and you'll be a light for someone else.

In the fuzzy early days there's just love. As it always should be. But later it can be tough — it can be daunting. The hardest things in life are the most important. That's OK — I promise we have all been there.

If your birth wasn't what you thought it would be, if it was awful and you're struggling to make sense of it all — there are mothers out there who have felt this too. I promise. You didn't do anything wrong, and it's not a sign of who you are as a parent. You are strong. You are not alone.

If you struggle with feeding, so many mothers have been there. And they've questioned what it means. You didn't fail. You can't fail — you love your baby and that's what matters.

If your baby won't gain weight and something is wrong — know that this path too has been walked by many mothers. They have left a trail of petals for you, wishes on stars, and silent hopes. They're carrying you in their heart and they want to help you through.

Whatever your path, it is a path walked by another mother who can hold your hand on your journey.

Your babies will grow like weeds and you'll be amazed at how fast it all went — but don't worry, you won't miss anything if you take time for you.

The kids will drive you mad. Their screaming will make you

feel like you want to run away. But you won't. Let yourself have a break. Have a wine or chocolate or binge-watch *Outlander*. You matter too. Don't let your light dim.

You'll do wonderfully, you're doing wonderfully.

Welcome to your home now.

Welcome home.

We're here for you, and soon you'll be nursing a coffee and watching your babies tearing around the house. You'll hear of a new baby born and your eyes will sting for just a moment.

Welcome, you'll whisper.

Welcome to the world, Mama.

An essential list of essential essentials for your new baby

BY EMILY WRITES

Having a baby is a wonderful time to spend all of the money you have. Once baby has arrived, they basically take care of themselves if you have all of the necessary hardware that goes with them. That's what this list is for. It can be confusing, knowing what you need and what you also need, so I thought I'd create a list for you. Thank me later, in the form of photos and GIFs of Alexander Skarsgård as Tarzan, Photoshopped to make it look like he wants to take me to his jungle, swing from my vines and bare his necessities to me, if you know what I mean (I mean fornication).

A BABY BLANKET KNITTED WITH ANTIQUE MOA HAIR MADE BY NARCOLEPTIC RACOONS FROM THE ANDES

Sure, a blanket from Kmart on special for $2.99 might be fine and less scratchy and less prone to weird kinkajou viruses. But you'll be the only one at coffee group without one and do you really want to deal with that kind of stigma? It will probably follow your child all the way through life, and when they go for a job the boss will be a baby from your coffee group and they'll say HOLD ON. MY MUM TOLD ME ABOUT YOU — YOU ARE THE KMART BLANKET BABY.

A PUNCHING BAG

Every time someone says 'Is she a good baby? Is she sleeping?' when you've had 10 minutes sleep in two days, you can punch the bag instead of your Great Aunt Ethel. When an old lady at the supermarket says your three-day old baby needs solids, you can punch the bag instead of getting arrested. When your partner pretends they're asleep WHEN YOU FUCKING KNOW THEY ARE NOT ASLEEP: go to the bag, punch the bag.

A WHITE-NOISE MACHINE

You need a white-noise machine to drown out the crying while you drink wine in the shower. It's not even for sleeping. LOL. SLEEP. AS IF! It's just a nice, calming backdrop for attempting to remember what it was like to shit by yourself.

8000 PAIRS OF SHOES THAT ONLY FIT YOUR BABY BEFORE THEY ACTUALLY START WALKING

The purpose of these shoes is for your baby to pull them off their feet and leave them around the house. Your baby cannot walk. Has no interest in walking. These are purely for decoration/inconvenience. They also have zero resale value. When you go to pack them away, as none of them fit your now-walking baby, half will be unworn and half will not be able to be paired up. When you move house, you will find under your couch six individual shoes that don't match.

AN $800 PAIR OF ERGONOMICALLY DESIGNED SHOES MADE BY A TEAM OF NASA SCIENTISTS SO THAT YOUR CHILD WILL WALK PROPERLY

Were you going to put them in normal shoes from The Warehouse for $4.50? No judgement, but you're a fucking monster.

A CAR SEAT THAT REAR-FACES UNTIL YOUR CHILD IS 37

It comes with a complementary smug response to use in Facebook groups when people have bought the wrong car seat.

SIX DIFFERENT THOMAS THE TANK ENGINE TRACKS THAT DO NOT MATCH EACH OTHER

This may seem like jumping the gun, considering you're only eight weeks pregnant, but it's never too early to buy overpriced shit that doesn't match and is just left all over your house to drive you crazy. Each track only costs about $16 million, and the good thing is your child will play with it for eight seconds and then say, 'The tracks don't match, I need the tracks that work'.

A BABY BOOK

For you to fill in until they're three months old. Then you'll just throw in random photos and vaccination cards and hope somehow the book fills in itself.

A NEVER-ENDING BOX OF TISSUES

You'll spend the next million years alternating between happy tears and sad tears and you won't want to change a thing even though everything is awful, because it's only awful for an hour or maybe a day or maybe a week if the walls are dripping with vomit. You'll need a box of tissues for late at night when you're grateful the kids are asleep so you can look at photos of them on your phone and think about how much you love them. You'll need a box of tissues for when you see someone you haven't seen for ages and they say 'What are your kids like?' and you start falling over your words — they're brilliant, hilarious, gentle, loving, kind, cheeky! They're the best thing that ever happened to me. They're my world. They're everything. Hand me a tissue.

The legend of the Relaxed Mother

BY GEORGINA LANGDON-POLE

Georgina Langdon-Pole is a writer, lecturer and community development practitioner passionate about social justice and giving a shit. She's also the proud mother of two tiny humans.

Gather around, ladies and gents. I am going to tell you the story of a magical sorceress. Legend calls her the 'Relaxed Mother.'

The myth of the Relaxed Mother is perpetuated by the Baby Whisperers, AKA visitors, AKA your great auntie's cousin's best-friend's neighbour. Shortly after I gave birth they came in their droves, bringing the smell of musty perfume and tales of the Relaxed Mother. Legend has it she can be found having a hypnotic birth beside a stream, or sitting happily in a deafening café just a few days after her birth. The high-pitched gushing seemed endless. 'Oh, she has SUCH a good baby. It must be because she's SUCH a Relaxed Mother,' they'd cluck, while I thought about more pressing matters like the fear of my first poo, or wondering if I'd ever leave the house again.

I wanted to meet this incredible woman. After the birth of my son I stumbled around the house in my nana nightie, anxious, covered in a thin layer of milk and baby pee. I cried on average once an hour. Sometimes for genuine reasons, like over my dishevelled vagina, or at the realisation I might never sleep again. Other times for stranger reasons, because — oh, I dunno — my partner made me peanut butter instead of Nutella toast, or I saw a dew-drop on a leaf in the garden.

I had every intention of being a Relaxed Mother. Smart-looking people in books told me that during labour, the more tense you are from the pain, the slower the cervix dilates. So I figured I'd just need to relax a bit, right? Like, take a chill pill, bro. Meditate. Go to my happy place. Think about fairies and butterflies and sunsets on beaches. This did not happen. Instead, I fantasised about getting a giant needle in my spine. Chanted for it like a possessed demon. When the anaesthetist arrived she was wearing normal, serious doctor clothes, but she may as well have been covered in gold and glitter with giant angel wings sprouting from her back. I was all like: 'YES!!! PLEASE PLEASE PLEASE CAN YOU STICK A GIANT NEEDLE INTO MY SPINE I WILL LOVE YOU FOREVER YOU ARE MY SAVIOUR!!!'

Post-birth, on my first outing to a café, I tried to breastfeed my baby. He wailed so loud you could barely hear the painful/repetitive/monotonous music overhead. I fumbled with my nipple shield (which made me look like a bit Madonna, only housewifey). Meanwhile, my breast hung out as milk projectiled directly into my baby's eye. At moments like these, appearances matter. You want to avoid the judgement that your being unable to calm your baby is a reflection of how uptight you are. Cue slightly concerned but relaxed look. Casual, nonchalant laughter. Keep calm; look at ease. Actual internal dialogue: 'Oh God, everyone is staring at me. What's wrong with you, you little shit! If you're hungry, just eat!'

Yes, I admit it. I have called my precious bundle of joy a little shit. This was usually followed by uncontrollable weeping. Out of guilt — but also because he had done something excruciatingly cute, like blinked, and it was so perfect and adorable and beautiful.

Those first few weeks are a roller-coaster ride, naked and without a seat belt. Unless you're a 1950s housewife who has developed a strong appetite for tea and codeine, most of us first-time mothers are not relaxed. We flick from extreme to extreme, calling our baby a dick one minute, then cradling them and sobbing, plotting never to leave their side before their twenty-first birthday, the next.

Not everyone understood this. Some Baby Whisperers gave me subtle (and by subtle I mean in-your-face), encouraging (and by encouraging I mean pushy) advice. The kind of advice followed by a stale smile, the smile that said: 'I am worried for you, Georgina. Worried you'll become a crazed hermit, breastfeeding your baby until he's sixteen.' Again and again, I was encouraged to just get on with life and be 'normal' again. And, in some other pre-mangled-genitalia, pre-night-is-the-new-day, pre-tiny-human dimension (THE PAST), I wanted this. But in the present? I didn't want to go out for a chai latte, while I sat there analysing how the trendy chair hurt my haemorrhoids. I wanted to curl up into a ball, crawl under my duvet and rock gently. I wanted to sit there, stare at my sleeping baby and weep because this tiny human was the embodiment of perfection. And because my vagina hurt. It hurt bad.

So who is this Relaxed Mother, this mysterious shape-shifting creature? She is that Barbie doll you played with when you were five, and that really together-looking person in the latest issue of *Woman's Day*. She is off over there in the distance riding her unicorn over a fucking rainbow. Real mothers are exactly that: real. Human. And, although they often come into the world looking like a cross between a sultana and a Martian, our babies are only human too. When they cry it is usually less a reflection of our mental state and more to do with the fact that we ate cabbage and bok choy for dinner.

I anticipate that there will be a few more concerned smiles before my son grows up. Because I'm too soft or too hard, or not relaxed enough. But if the cry of my baby didn't make my brain pulse and my heart race, I'd probably be sitting in the bath with a whisky while my toddler graffitied the lounge walls with his faeces. I might accidentally take the wrong child home from the park, or even worse: the odd socks would never be found. I am happy to let the Relaxed Mother ride her unicorn off into the distance. I'll be the one in the car park, swearing at my stroller as I try to assemble it. I'll be right here on planet Earth, being human, thank you very much.

Translating the crap we say at coffee group about our kids

BY EMILY WRITES

Being a parent is hard. Sometimes we lie to make it feel like it's easier. It's not a mean-spirited lie. It's a fib to help us cope. There are no performance reviews in parenting, yet it often feels like a competition. Of course, we know it's really not — but there are so many competiparents about it can be hard not to fall into the trap. Especially when you feel like you're coming in last.

So, of course there will be times when you say something that stretches the truth just a smidge.

I no longer go to coffee groups. I found them to be a bit too much of a challenge. It wasn't necessarily the other mothers, it was the pressure I put on myself. They — those clean and calm other mothers — seemed to have it all, and have it all together. I felt a bit like I was in need of being performance-managed out of this, the best job there is.

I know now, having been a mum for four years, that nobody really has it all together.

But in those days, well, with a new baby I felt like I was being judged no matter what I did. I wanted it to seem like I wasn't falling apart and I didn't want anyone to know. So sometimes I said things that needed a translation, a dictionary of Coffee Mum to Real Mum phrases. And they went something like this:

Oh yes, we have a very strong bond.
Translation: He won't let me out of his sight, including at night, so I get no fucking sleep.

It's a very, very strong bond.
Translation: He likes to watch me poop. And I let him.

He's adventurous.
Translation: He got stuck halfway under the fridge once and I had to use butter to get him out again. Please assure me that's normal.

He's a talker.
Translation: Can you hear me over the sound of his relentless screaming?

He's very independent.
Translation: Just this morning he told me I'm not his best friend, will never be his best friend, and never have ever *ever* been his best friend.

He's a problem solver.
Translation: He moved a chair to cover the hole he put in the wall because he had head-butted it just to see what would happen if he head-butted a wall.

He's very advanced.
Translation: He farted once and it gave him such a fright he cried for an hour. Your child is already saying hello in three different languages so I need to say *something*, OK?

He's bilingual.
Translation: He watches 12 hours of *Peppa Pig* a day so he has a British accent.

He keeps me on my toes!
Translation: I haven't slept in four years and sometimes I talk to my wine.

I agree — breastfeeding is really wonderful, isn't it?
Translation: I have mastitis and this is literally the worst thing I've ever done in my life. If you say breastfeeding is easy one more time I will punch you square in the face.

I know, so much judgement! I never judge other mums.
Translation: You literally just said you don't work because you don't want anybody else to raise your kids. You literally just said that. Also your top is ugly. I know it's designer, but it's ugly.

My husband and I are closer than ever since we had kids.
Translation: The other night we fought for two hours about who ate the last Trumpet. HOW COULD HE EAT IT WHEN IT WAS MINE.

Yeah, I don't drink much these days either.
Translation: I haven't had a drink yet and it's 10 a.m., so sure.

I miss my kids when they're at kindy, too!
Translation: I do not.

Yeah, they're going to stay at their nana's tonight and I'm going to miss them so much!
Translation: I am not.

Mine sleeps through the night, too.
Translation: If through the night you mean never.

Oh I know, screen time is terrible.
Translation: I have had sexual fantasies about *Fireman Sam*.

I am grateful! I am literally cherishing moments so hard I am in agony.
Translation: Can we be real? Please. Read my mind.

After playing this game for a few months, I met a woman who answered differently. She set up the 'I'm loving this, every single second, every minute, aren't you?' trap and I agreed that yes, I was loving it, every single second, every minute, of course. Then she burst into tears. We walked outside the shitty Plunket rooms and looked at the grass that hadn't been mowed in months.

It's so hard, she said.

It is, I said.

She never stops crying, she said.

I feel like I can't give either of them enough time. They want me so much, I said.

This isn't what I thought it would be, she said.

Same, I said. I thought two would be easier than this.

I can't cope with one, she said.

But you are! I said. Look at you! You're dressed and out of the house. You're here.

She smiled. I smiled. We hugged. We sat on the concrete.

Two new friends. We had broken the barrier. Thrown the dictionary away. We were two mums really talking now.

We met again the next day. And again and again. Cold coffee and warm homes. Talking and talking and talking until suddenly it was hours later. We decided we needed to make a promise to always tell the truth. We talked to more mums and we stopped ourselves from falling into fibs.

If we're judged, we're judged. If we're seen as bad mums, then so be it. We have each other, and we have others and suddenly we have a community. In the truth is the beauty of parenting. It's hard. It's wonderful. It's too good to be true, and too hard to make up.

We don't need a translator, we need each other.

Babies and time: The stolen and beloved minutes, weeks, days, nights and years

BY THOMASIN SLEIGH

Thomasin Sleigh is a writer with a focus on contemporary art and culture who has written for galleries and magazines throughout Australasia. Her debut novel Ad Lib *was published in 2014.*

MINUTES

A pregnancy test. Wait. You have to wait two minutes before you look at the slender lines. Lines which signify a new human being. Inside of you. Holy shit. You could be anywhere: sitting on your friend's bathroom floor; on the toilet at home (it's a sunny Saturday and outside you can hear your neighbour mowing their berm — they were a baby once, they started out as a collision of cells inside another person, and now look at them, absorbed in trimming their berm); or you could be in a flimsy cubicle at work, a plastic wand sitting on top of a metal toilet-paper dispenser.

Don't look at it. You have to wait two minutes.

Those two minutes warp and stretch out ahead of you. They are minutes made up of innocent seconds, but those seconds pass with a syrupy slowness. What else is there to look at? Only the grey walls and the fluorescent light above you. You check your phone and it's only been one minute, but you look at the test anyway: a blue cross. Starkly conclusive. But is it really true, this obdurate blue cross, since you haven't waited the stipulated two minutes? A cross is a new person, so it's important to get this right. You stare at it, absorbing this equation. Someone comes into the cubicle next to you; the door clangs closed, and you hear the thin trickle of their pee.

WEEKS

These two minutes are followed by the unit of weeks. There is the primary question: how many weeks along are you? Forty weeks is the deadline you are moving towards. The weeks are broken down into trimesters: week 12, week 27, week 40. How do you visualise the time? A grid? A dotted line? A flip chart? Perhaps you are synesthetic, and the trimesters each have their own colour. The first trimester could be a dusty pink, an internal pink, the pink of the imagined activity in your uterus, or the inside of a cat's mouth.

However the time appears, of more pressing concern is how many weeks until you stop feeling sick. The prognoses vary. Some women are sick for 12 weeks, some are sick for 40, some are sick for zero weeks. Being sick is purportedly a good sign because it means that you are filled with hormones and your body is doing what it needs to do for your baby to grow. This is a good sign, you tell yourself, when you are throwing up in your mum's garden, next to the emergent dahlias.

You come to realise that pregnancy is holding two contradictory positions simultaneously: a good sign manifests itself in feeling awful, and every moment of elation has a shadow of worry. Similarly, time moves both fast and slow, the days of sickness are clouded and inch by, and then suddenly you are 40 weeks pregnant and the baby is arriving *today*.

DAYS

Why isn't the baby here today? Your due date has been so firm and understandable throughout the pregnancy, a nice tidy number around which you could organise your life: when you were supposed to stop feeling sick, when you would finish work, when your mum would come down and meet the baby. Now, the date drifts away behind you like a lost hat and every new day unspools ahead of you. Lying in bed in the morning you are faced with two possibilities: today could be the day you produce a new human being, or today could be the day you wipe down the sticky shelves under the kitchen sink.

At a check-up with the midwife, you listen to the baby's heartbeat inside of you, its squelchy pulse measuring out the seconds. The baby is counting too. Sometimes the baby hiccups and this strikes up a counterpoint: one, two, one, two. 'Any day now,' the midwife says. Any day. But not today, or today, or today.

NON-TIME

And then you're in labour and you're counting again. The time between the contractions is just as important as the contractions themselves. It's like a trompe-l'oeil image which shows two wine glasses or two faces looking at each other, depending on which way you look at it — once again, two contradictory positions. Except the labour is a lot more painful than a trompe-l'oeil image. It's a new pain; it has dips and spaces and jagged edges and the contractions roll through you. Would the pain be as bad if the space in between didn't exist? If it were one unending plateau of pain? It's hard to conceive of any person being able to contend with such unremitting agony. The time in between is both a rest and a terror, because you know the next contraction will arrive and you can't escape it.

In the deepest, darkest place of labour, there is no time. There are others who will tell you with confidence: 'It was two hours' or, 'It took half an hour.' But there is no time in this place. There are no other people. There is just your body, the relentless logic of the contractions, and the spaces in between. Like a Morse code of pain: long, short, long, short, long . . .

NO HISTORY

Your baby appears and it has no history. It has been inside of you, waiting to emerge, accumulating its in-utero weeks, where your time and its time were inextricable. But now, here, screaming and slimy, it is beginning its very own timeline, distinct from you and your body. Your lives are two parallel lines which will never again meet.

If you want to run with a metaphor, then the baby is a watch and its organs are its cogs, and now that the baby is its own being, they are all starting up. The circulatory system kicks into gear and the lungs fill with their first breaths of air. Valves are closing in the heart and blood is flowing in different directions. The heart chugs blood through its new channels, the metronome of the baby's life.

NIGHTS AND DAYS

The baby, having been buoyant in the darkness of your womb, sees no distinction between night and day. Your previous twenty-four hour patterns are upended and take on new meanings and structures. Six o'clock in the evening isn't a time for a glass of wine and sitting on the couch, it is one of the most intense times of the day: the baby cries and feeds, and cries and feeds, and refuses to sleep. Eight-thirty on Sunday morning isn't a time for sleeping in or finishing your book: the baby is awake and needs something from you: a feed, a change, a burp, or to grip tightly to your index finger with its delicate but firm hand.

When you were at work, the Tetris-like blocks of your Outlook calendar may have determined your day's structure, but now the days are mapped around the baby's naps. The baby falls asleep. Time check: 10.30. You probably have 45 minutes to get something done, have a shower, empty the dishwasher or work on your essay about babies and time. The day is dispensed to you in small parcels of baby-sleeping time, and larger parcels of baby-awake time, when the baby drools and wriggles its new body around.

The baby's cries wake you in the night. As you drag yourself awake, rising up from the depths of your sleep, the big question rises within you: what time is it? The answer sort of matters, and sort of doesn't. It matters because you either had a life-saving three hours sleep, or it's only been 20 minutes since you carefully laid the sleeping baby down, slowly, slowly, so as not to wake it. But it doesn't matter as well, because you have to do the same things, regardless of the time. You need to check the baby, feed it, cuddle it, change its nappy, and repeat, and repeat — keep clicking through the spin cycle of the newborn.

YEARS

After the baby is born, you use days to tell other people your baby's age, then you say the weeks, then the months, and then your baby has accumulated a whole year, and this becomes the most useful unit for measuring a human's existence.

What if we continued to use days to determine how old we are? This person is 11,680 days old. Or weeks? This person is 1668 weeks old. The numbers are too big and ungainly; there's no way we could keep track of the rapidly amassing time. As you age, the detail of hours and days drifts away and it is easier to pin events to the arc of a whole year. 'That was the year that I had that terrible hair cut,' you might think. Or, 'We got together some time in 2003.'

But when the baby is just starting out, at the very beginning, every day is significant and no other unit of measurement will do. 'He's just ten days old,' you say when your aunt comes to visit, and you both look down at the baby, swaddled and calm, its eyelids a soft pink. 'You'll blink,' your aunt says, 'and he'll be eighteen and finishing school. It happens too fast. You need to appreciate this time, because it is gone before you know it.' It's easy to feel this appreciation when the baby is feeding contentedly and you reach out and stroke the downy hair on its head. It's harder at three o'clock in the morning when the baby spews in your bed.

How does such a small, vulnerable creature have such a radically disruptive effect on time? There are periods when the baby is like an outboard motor, rocketing both of you into the future, it's suddenly Friday and the week has disappeared through your fingers. Then there are periods when time stutters, stalls, and slinks by; the baby has fallen asleep on you after a feed and you sit and watch its sleeping face. As your aunt suggested, you blink, and when you open your eyes the baby is still there. It isn't 18 years old, it's just a little baby with a plump milk-drunk face; a small, sleeping clock; a human reminder of the passing of time.

The story of a mum (who tried her best but needed a rest)

BY ELIZA PRESTIDGE OLDFIELD

Eliza Prestidge Oldfield is a mum of two and lawyer, living in Wellington.

Once upon a time there was a little boy who was almost three and sometimes he could be diabolical.

One day he found an interesting bag of something sparkly at the bottom of the art supplies box.

He asked his mum, what is it?

And his mum (who tried her best but needed a rest) said, it's glitter, even though it wasn't really glitter, it was that stuff like coloured bits of torn foil paper.

No sooner had she said this than the baby tried to grab the bag and some spilled and it started to get Very Messy. So the mum (who tried her best but needed a rest) said maybe it was a big-boy game better for when the baby was asleep.

And everything was OK for a while, because they played

with something else.

But things were about to get *much* worse.

Because later that afternoon when the baby was asleep they got the glitter out again.

The mum (who tried her best but needed a rest and was sometimes over-ambitious) put some double-sided tape on some cardboard and showed the little boy how to put the cardboard in a dish of glitter and make sparkly pictures. She taught him how to sprinkle it back into the dish, making lovely glittery rain. And everything was OK for a while, because they were having fun.

But things were about to get *much* worse.

Because the baby woke up. And the mum (who tried her best but needed a rest and was sometimes a complete idiot) said, OK you stay here and I'll try to get your brother back to sleep.

Well.

The baby would not go back to sleep, and so the mum tried to feed him some milk, but then the little boy (who was almost three and could be quite diabolical), ran up all excited and said **LOOK AT ME I AM YOVELY AND CLITTERY**. And the mum (who tried her best but needed a rest and was actually fairly patient) said oh my gosh, you are very glittery, back in your room now while I feed your brother, eh? And everything was OK for a while because the boy went back to his room.

But things were about to get *much* worse.

Because he came back out again with a handful of glitter and he threw it at the baby. And the mum (who tried her best but needed a rest and was fucked off by this attack) said **NO NO NO HE DOESN'T LIKE THAT GO BACK TO YOUR ROOM UNTIL HE HAS FINISHED HIS MILK**.

And everything was OK for a while because the boy went back to his room.

But things were about to get *much* worse.

Because the boy came back with another handful of glitter and threw it on his mum and his baby brother again.

And his mum (who tried her best but needed a rest and hasn't yet figured out effective chaos-management techniques for her child) put him in his room and shut the door and went to another room and shut that door too and tried to feed the baby.

And everything was OK for a while because the baby stopped crying.

But things were about to get *much* worse.

Because the boy opened both the doors and came out with a very big handful of glitter and threw it right in the baby's face. And the mum (who tried her best but fuck it what does that even mean? It's been eight long months since the baby was born and this is still a day-to-day failure) said OH FOR THE LOVE OF GOD WHAT THE FUCK, KID! THAT IS REALLY ANNOYING AND INCONSIDERATE. LOOK. HE IS CRYING. LOOK YOU MADE HIM CRY. HE DOESN'T LIKE THAT AT ALL. YOU NEED TO RESPECT HIS BOUNDARIES.

And the boy ran away laughing and jumped on the couch, leaving a trail of glitter everyfuckingwhere and sending showers of glitter all through the lounge with every jump.

And everything was not OK but the mum (who tried her best but needed a stiff fucking drink) wanted to make it OK so she got the vacuum cleaner out, but the baby started crying as soon as she put him in his exersaucer, and the boy was still running around the house throwing glitter everywhere and so she said FUCK IT. WE'RE GOING OUT. GO STAND BY THE DOOR AND WAIT FOR ME WHILE I GET THINGS READY.

And everything was still not OK and the mum (who tried her best but was completely ropable) said DO YOU HEAR ME. GO WAIT FOR ME BY THE DOOR. WE'RE GOING OUT.

And then everything was OK for a while because they went to Te Papa and the boy played independently and the baby crawled around and the mum vented on Twitter.

But things were about to get *much* worse.

Because the baby started to gag and splutter and go purple. And the mum (who tried her best but was a bit panicked over what he might have eaten on the floor) hooked her finger into his mouth and pulled out . . . a piece of fucking foil glitter.

And then everything was OK for a while because the baby didn't die.

But things were about to get worse again, although the baby almost choking is the peak of the bad things, so let's chill a bit about the rest of it.

Because then they went home. And the house was still covered in glitter. And the mum (who tried her best and felt like this whole thing should have been filmed and shown in schools to promote responsible contraception use) put the boy at the table with *Doc McStuffins* on the laptop and the baby in the highchair with a Cruskit and tried to get some dinner organised.

And everything was OK for a while because it was almost 6.30 p.m. and surely the boy's dad would be home soon and then he could corral the children and the glitter clean-up could begin.

But things were about to get worse.

Because she called the dad and he was only just running to the bus stop. So she yelled **WHAT THE FUCK. YOU HAVE GOT TO BE KIDDING ME** and hung up.

And everything was not OK because the house was absolute glitter chaos.

But even so, things were about to get worse.

Because the mum (who tried her best and figured she'd better clean this shit up), got the vacuum cleaner out, and the baby started howling, and then the boy did a wee in his trousers, and the mum said ARRRGGGHHHHHHHHHH WHY IS THIS MY LIFE?!

And the mum decided to put the boy in the corner of the lounge with the least glitter and set up more *Doc McStuffins* while she cleaned up. And she put the baby in the decorative but uncomfortable baby carrier purchased on a holiday in Vietnam in freer times when the children were not yet born, and vacuumed up some of the glitter while carrying the baby.

And everything was OK because this was sort of working.

But it was about to get worse again because then she vacuumed up a fucking baby sock and fuck it, why are the fucking socks always fucking everywhere?

Then the dad came home and that was a blessing, and the mum unblocked the sock and then spent FORTY-FIVE MINUTES vacuuming the house and getting glitter off the floors.

And then everything was OK because the boys were bathed and almost dressed and the floors were vacuumed and it was almost bedtime.

But then the mum (who was holding on by the barest of threads, awaiting the blissful moment when the children fell asleep) realised that the boy had got glitter all through his bed and that still wasn't cleaned up.

The moral of this story, friends, is that if your mother-in-law gives you some glitter foil stuff for your kids to do art with, you should throw it in the bin immediately.

Biological roulette: Coping after birth goes seriously wrong

BY FRANCESCA JONES

Francesca Jones is a New Zealander who has somehow spent most of her adult life living in Europe and Australia. When she is not busy wrangling her two children she writes on her blog, My Flatpack Life.

Please be aware that this story is an account of birth trauma and contains a graphic depiction of a near-fatal birth.

∼

I held my daughter after she was born, for a few minutes. I don't remember it.

I wonder, is there a difference between holding your child and not knowing it happened, and not holding your child at all?

I remember the midwife, at the head of my bed, noticing the

placenta was about to be delivered. It is my last clear memory. This snapshot sits in my head because something jolted in my brain — *pay attention, something is about to go wrong* — like your senses springing to life as they see the headlights driving towards you. I am the proverbial possum, frozen, helpless, but alert. Then the slam of impact. The feeling. The feeling I have no words for.

The placenta is delivered intact. Something comes with it that is not supposed to. Something that is supposed to stay inside my body. My uterus.

Like peeling off a sock from the top down, or reaching in to your pocket and pulling it out. My uterus is turned inside out, and is suddenly a very external organ. A uterine inversion; a rare complication of labour. Most obstetricians will go their whole careers without seeing one.

The uterus cannot contract like it should, and without the placenta against it the blood has nowhere to go but the bed, the floor. The blood loss is rapid. I will lose 3.7 litres in total. My blood pressure plunges, out of proportion to the blood loss. I am raced to theatre.

My husband is left alone in the delivery suite. This is how he holds our daughter for the first time. Lying down, cradling our daughter to his chest. He waits for someone to come back and tell him how I am, what has happened to me.

Eventually he rings his parents, and then my father. I do not know what he said to them. All I can imagine of these conversations is the silences, and the moment his voice cracks.

Down the hall, I am in and out of consciousness. A swarm of medical staff surround me, vague shapes outside the bright lights I am exposed under. Needles. Nausea. My body shaking uncontrollably on the table.

My next clear memory is this: a midwife talking to me once

I am stable. She tells me they will move me soon. That they will bring my daughter to me.

My daughter.

Those words slam into me with an almost physical force. The child I had held inside me for nine months was no longer there. My arms were supposed to be cradling my child, not strapped to an operating table. Where was she? Was she crying? How much did she weigh? Would I even be able to hold her?

I could. In recovery they lay my daughter on my chest. I remember a huge feeling of peace at getting to hold my child. Nurses had put a hat on my daughter. I had a vague memory of black baby hair. I remember desperately wanting to feel that hair against my chest, but was too weak to ask. Words were beyond me.

―

Just as there is no real preparation for the reality of labour, there is no preparation for an experience like mine. I still firmly believe that, in general, women can and should be better prepared for situations where birth does not go according to plan. Women go to classes, and read books. Over and over again we are told that birth is a natural event, that it is nothing to be afraid of. We are told to stay relaxed, our bodies know what to do. This is true, in the vast majority of cases. There is almost a reluctance to discuss potential complications, as though by talking about them we will make them happen. Despite this, when things do go wrong, we were meant to have seen it coming. Birth is a risky business, we are now told. Was it our fault — for not relaxing enough, or having the temerity to write a birth plan?

I am certain I was not naïve in my preparation for my

daughter's birth. She is my second child and I had experienced serious complications with my first birth. My son had spent some time in special care, too. I had been hoping that this time I would not haemorrhage, that this time I would get to hold my newborn.

Instead, I found myself weak and desperately sick. Confined to a hospital bed. My husband and daughter roomed in with me. He did everything for her: rocked her in his arms, changed her, fed her. The nurses were in and out of the room, a stream of monitors and intravenous (IV) lines. I watched, like it was all a show for an audience of one. I waited for people to lay my daughter on my chest. I didn't actually 'hold' my daughter in my arms until she was three days old. Even then my arms had to be supported by pillows.

I was carrying a different weight. One I couldn't share. The burden of my experience.

Be grateful.

In the immortal words of Emily Writes: I am grateful — now fuck off.

I am grateful to be alive, in a way that — unless you too have teetered on that great divide — you may not be able to understand. It does me no kindness to remind me of this gratefulness. The enormity of what did not happen is too big. The potential loss — the loss of everything. Not just the lost memory of holding my daughter. The loss of every moment that would follow it. My daughter and my son. Healthy and growing but lost to me forever.

I am grateful my daughter was fine. She is now a healthy, thriving toddler. What happened is about me, not her. She is an entirely separate thing. These are not selfish thoughts. So as much as I understand the impulse to say them, these words hurt:

You forget the pain once you hold your baby.

As long as my child is healthy it will be worth it.

Or — hardest of all for me to hear — I would have done anything for it to be me.

These words are a door slamming in my face. Once they are in a conversation, how do I join in? If I could find the words I would want to say this: I'm sorry for what your baby went through, but I would not wish what happened to me on anyone either.

The grief women like me feel is real. Too often we are made to feel that as long as our babies are healthy we have nothing to complain about. Too often we are silenced before we can express the devastating toll our bodies and minds have suffered. We are helpless before the rolling maul of advice and internet commentary. The hilarious horror stories. The endless extolling of the 'golden hour'. Hold your baby for the first hour of its life: it will promote mother-baby bonding, it will improve your chance of successfully breastfeeding, it will help stabilise your baby's temperature and heart rate. Holding your baby will make them feel secure in this transition to life outside the womb. So we haven't just missed out, we have also failed on page one of all of the 'caring for your newborn' books.

Women who experience a traumatic birth (whether that is one physically traumatic like mine, or mentally, via loss of control and bodily autonomy, or due to medical complications their baby experienced) are vulnerable to postnatal mood disorders, whether that is depression, anxiety or post-traumatic stress disorder (PTSD). I had nightmares and flashbacks for months. I still cannot walk into a hospital without feeling dread in the pit of my stomach and my heart pounding in my chest.

We can, and should, support women like me better. We need to acknowledge that things can and do go suddenly wrong. That this is not because of something the mother has done. It is just biological roulette. When things do go wrong, we need to support women who are struggling. We need to acknowledge their grief, and not dismiss it. I was able to go back to hospital to discuss what had happened. I was even able to see the operating theatre I was taken to. This helped enormously in being able to come to terms with what I remembered. In cases like mine, talking amongst our friends is not enough — we need the medical profession involved to help us make sense of what we experienced.

I am proof that modern medicine is an amazing thing. That when things do go catastrophically wrong doctors and nurses can cope.

I am grateful for this.

But, sometimes, when my daughter cries in the night and I go to her, I pick her up and feel her hair against my cheek and say 'It's OK, Mama's here.'

I wonder who I am trying to comfort. Her, or me?

Dispatches from a long night featuring vomit

BY EMILY WRITES

The night shift started with an attempt to write something and ignore the pitter-patter of feet on the stairs. I knew they belonged to my four-year-old. He knew he was meant to be in bed.

He poked his head around the top of the stairs and said 'Oh . . . hi Mama!' as if he was thinking: Fancy seeing you here!

'You're meant to be in bed,' I told him. He insisted 'Deddy' said he could stay up 'for how ever I want, maybe even all night acshully!'

I picked up my phone and said, 'Oh shall we ask Daddy?' to which he replied, 'Oh no, bedder not, it's our secret maybe?'

Of course. So we sat together and I made attempts to write and he sighed theatrically because I wouldn't let him watch TV and he was 'VEWY BORED!' over and over again until, losing the will to live, I said fine.

Fine, fine, *fine* — I gave up all attempts at productivity and scooped him up and carried him downstairs.

'Maybe just sleep in bed with me because we're best friends' he said. So I lay down next to him and fell asleep within 3.2 seconds and I assume he did too because I didn't wake up until my husband yelled 'PUKE!' from the baby's room.

I was so disorientated to wake up in a bunk that I immediately nailed myself on the roof of the bed. Then I stepped onto Duplo, which was at least not Lego, not-so-silently cursing that I hadn't made more of an effort to get my oldest to clean his room. But his idea of cleaning is just to pull more shit out and not put away all of the other shit.

I turned on the light in the baby's room to see my husband catching spew in his hand. I was still waking up so it took me a second to grab a towel as the vomit dripped through his fingers. I scooped up the baby and pulled off his top, which was now covered in puke. My husband's back gave out as he tried to get up from the slippery, vomit-covered bed. He lay groaning in the sick as the baby began to giggle. A sleepy Eddie turned up at the door — 'Why'd you do sick out your mouf?' he asked me.

I tried to dress the baby who was now farting with increasing intensity.

'I'm worried he's going to shit everywhere so just — I'm going to re-do his nappy now,' I said to my husband, who was face down on the mattress and not really able to contribute other than to make increasingly desperate I'm-in-pain noises. Eddie climbed onto his father's back. 'Your becks OK Deddy?'

'Get off and go back to sleep right now,' I said as I changed the baby's nappy.

'Maybe I will do all I want,' he said — chin jutting out — before resting his head on his father's hunched back. Despite puking a HUGE AMOUNT the baby was wriggling and refusing to stay still.

'BED,' I said in my sternest I'm Your Mother voice.

'I can't — there's a poo in my bed.'

'WHAT? DID YOU POO IN YOUR BED? YOU DID NOT POO IN YOUR BED. YOU DID NOT.' I hissed at him as the baby laughed.

Eddie laughed too. 'I did a trick!'

'WHAT TRICK?' I said. 'DID YOU POO IN YOUR BED?'

'No, I trick you!' The baby laughed. I heard my husband's muffled laugh from the bed. The baby farted. My oldest tried to match his fart then rushed to the toilet.

'It's like 3 a.m. or something, can everyone just stop and—'

The baby vomited again.

I cleaned the baby up again.

I put a blanket over my broken husband after helping him into our bed.

I put the four-year-old back in the bed (after checking there was no poo).

And I climbed into the baby's bed with the baby.

The baby wrapped his sticky and hot arms around me and gave me a wet kiss. He slobbered over my cheeks then fell asleep, his face inches from mine.

The room smelled like vomit.

The vomit looked like porridge.

And I suddenly realised I was hungry.

Then I wondered just how desensitised I was to vomit that the sight of it didn't make me retch but instead made me wonder what I'd have for breakfast.

I hope I don't get sick, I thought to myself as the baby curled into me, trying to get under my skin. He was close enough to give me mouth to mouth.

Immediately my brain went into overdrive:

Was I going to get sick? I felt my tummy rumble. Oh, there it is. I'm going to get sick. I'm going to have to cancel the book event. What if I don't cancel and everyone gets the shits? It feels like the same nausea that I had when I was pregnant. Ugh, I hated being pregnant. Oh God, what if I'm pregnant? There's no way I'm pregnant. There's no way. But contraception fails, right? Yes, but I definitely can't be. What if I'm one of those women who just has a baby on the toilet? I don't want a toilet baby. I mean, I don't want another baby, let alone a toilet baby that I have no stuff for. I mean, I'm sure I'd work it out and it would be fine. I mean, I love babies. I mean, my babies are adorable and the baby is sleeping slightly better and I mean, he did just puke all through the bed, but I mean, they're so beautiful when they're sleeping. God, what is wrong with me? Do I want another child? No, I do not. But they're gorgeous. And if I just accidentally had a toilet baby because I was one of those 10 per cent of women that spontaneously has a contraceptive failure then I would love my toilet baby. And I could totally have three kids. I mean, by the time the third was born my first two would be sleeping through the night. I know that I thought this with my second and I ended up not sleeping for four years but I mean, what's another few months, right? Everything could change. I could love a toilet baby.

A gentle fart scattered my thoughts. The baby stretched out across the bed, his puku still round despite the chundering session.

Please don't let me get gastro, I thought. Please don't let me puke during a reading. Please don't let me give new mums the shits. Puking or shitting myself on camera is one of my greatest fears about doing media. Oh my God, what if I shit myself during a reading? Why was I laying in a bed marinated in baby vom? If he puked again I'd hear from the other room, wouldn't I? No, it was safer to stay in here, just in case.

The baby tested out some of his favourite co-sleeping positions:

The Who Put This Fucking Plank Here: Ram-rod straight in the middle of the bed. Horizontal. I can move him in this position and it's like he's levitating.

The Donald Trump: He kicks me in the face and then just as I'm starting to recover from being kicked in the face he kicks me in the face again.

The #blessed: He leaks out his nappy in the middle of the bed.

The Tarantino: When he tries to get both of his feet into my mouth.

Christian lobby group Family First NZ: When he farts in a continuous stream until he wakes himself up shitting.

Eventually I was forced to lay against the wall with his feet in the small of my back. But there was no more vomit so I was at peace. I drifted off and had a terrifying dream about Kiefer Sutherland riding a killer whale.

I woke up to a little voice. It was 5 a.m.

'Can I pee on him like on the holidays?' the four-year-old asked. His hair was messy and his eyes tired.

'No, that was a special occasion. You can only pee on someone if they've been stung by a jellyfish'.

I decided not to get into other reasons for peeing on someone. He looked at me with sad eyes.

'One day can I do wees on my brovver again?'

'Maybe. I just . . . It's super early in the morning, OK?'

'Anything can happen, you said, when we have dreams.'

Yeah OK. I did say that but I was hoping you'd strive for more than just pissing on your brother again.

'Why is your face like that?' he said.

'Like what?'

'Like old.'

'You and your brother made my face like this.'

He climbed onto my chest and smoothed my brow.

'Your face is my favourite one.'

Top tips for getting your baby to sleep

BY EMILY WRITES

Getting your baby to go to sleep is quite simple. All you need to do is change your diet, their diet, your environment, your lifestyle, and be prepared to rid yourself of everything you hold dear.

But this will work: if you follow these simple 627 instructions, your baby will be sleeping through the night every night except when they're teething, sick, wet, dry, bored, hungry, not hungry, lonely, questioning their existence, upset, not upset, tired or happy.

* The best way to get your child to sleep is to accept that they will never sleep. What does sleep really mean? Is it a metaphysical concept from which we truly need to wake?

* Have you considered a night light? Have you considered six night lights? Have you considered syncing them so that they simulate a gentle lightning storm in Denmark?

* Help your child to understand the difference between daytime and night-time by repeating IT IS DAYTIME IT IS

DAYTIME IT IS DAYTIME IT IS DAYTIME over and over and over and over and over again between the hours of 7 a.m. and 7 p.m. At 7 p.m., begin chanting **IT IS NIGHT-TIME IT IS NIGHT-TIME IT IS NIGHT-TIME.** You only need to do this between the hours of 7 p.m. and 7 a.m. for around one to eight years.

* Have you considered getting a product that can act as a security item for your child? How about an axe with the blade dulled slightly? This will help them feel safe at night. Or you could purchase a succubus to crouch at the end of their cot. Most succubi can be summoned at 3 a.m. if you stand inside a circle made from the blood of three virgins from Hamilton. Or you can hire them from the 'succubus' section on HomeHelp.com.

* Read *The Iliad* to your child. In Homeric Greek.

* Babies need to understand and organise their innate circadian rhythms. Spend three days collecting cicadas. Do not eat or sleep. This is an endurance test, and how you approach it will dictate your worth as a mother. Do not give in until you have at least 600 cicadas. Train them to play tiny instruments and teach them gentle lullabies like 'Run to the Hills' by Iron Maiden. When your cicada metal orchestra is complete, have it perform for your baby every night between the hours of 8 p.m. and 11.45 p.m. They'll be tired. They're cicadas. They're not used to this kind of thing. You're going to need to champion them. Lift their spirits. You can do this, cicada mama.

* Avoid coffee. If at all possible, try to get your baby onto decaf. Also, most class A drugs have caffeine in them, just something to keep in mind.

* Attempt, if you can, to halt the Earth's gravitational pull. It can impact the sleep patterns of your baby.

* Try some hypnotherapy — when you see your baby, tell them they're getting very sleepy. After you hypnotise them, resist the urge to get them to make goat noises for your (and your friends') entertainment.

* Rent a cruise liner. The soft rocking motion of being on the open sea may assist your baby in settling and staying asleep. If this isn't possible, consider moving onto a boat or small dinghy. Or sleep in the bath.

* Put your child to bed awake and they will fall asleep on their own. If they don't I don't know why, because that's what they're meant to do, apparently. All babies are the same, so they're all meant to sleep if you just follow the definitely not contradictory or made-up advice you see online. Maybe take your baby back to the hospital and ask if they can check the factory settings.

Four

BY EMILY WRITES

It was dark and I heard a little whimper then: 'Mama?'
   A little body quickly climbed into my bed and huddled up closer reaching for my hands. I pulled my arms around him and softly stroked his hair.
   I saw a shadow.
   It's OK baby you're safe.
   Can I come in bed even when I'm four if I see a shadow an is a scary man?
   Of course.
   Can you tell me a story so I don't cry?
   I was tired. But he was almost four.
   What story?
   A story about a monkey been my best friend.
   I whispered into the dark about the little monkey who wants to be best friends with the little boy. They build a house of flowers. They're always safe.
   The story ends the same every time.
   You finish it — Mama is tired, I say.
   An den that little boy found his mama and she carried him up the big hill to the house and she cuddled him to sleep.
   Goodnight baby, I said and a short silence followed and then . . .

Even if the boy is four does he keep his mama?

Yes.

Even if the boy is . . . he struggled to free his fingers to hold up six or maybe eight — finally ten . . . this many?

Yes. Go to sleep.

He wants to be a big boy but he fears it.

And tomorrow he will be four.

He wants big boy clothes and big boy toys, but he also wants cuddles in the night.

He wants adventures — pirates and monkeys and houses of flowers but he wants his mama to carry him up the hill when his legs are tired.

And today was his last day as three.

He wants to DO IT MYSELF but he wants the crook of my arm, my shoulder, the space under my ear, the arch of my back, his hand in mine.

I try to reassure him that 'four' isn't a threshold to cross where everything changes. It's just another day but on this particular day the answer to 'how old are you?' is a new one. And every time you say it, it's a little less new.

But it's a hard concept for an almost four-year-old to fathom.

And I'm not good at explaining. Because I look at that little button nose and the flushed red cheeks and the golden locks and the pointy knees and the little ears, and I fall over myself trying to say what four is.

Four is: How did you get so tall when I remember saying to your father 'quick, quick — now' and he would rush to me and put both hands on my belly. He wanted to feel you move and now you run between his legs and climb him like a little monkey on a tree.

Four is: Folding you up like origami so I can hold you in my arms like I did when you were born and when I put you in a sling and sang to you as I walked around the kitchen.

Four is: Trying not to laugh when you flail around dramatically demoting me of best friend status at any given moment. And trying not to be too pleased when you say, 'I didn't mean so, you are my bes fren'.

Four is: Trying not to cry when I drop you off at kindy and you say **PLEASE MAMA I MISS YOU.** I miss you too, don't you know? I'd rather have you on my knee but there are bills that must be paid.

Four is: Trying not to curse everything when you tell me other kids have been mean and there are all these rules about clothes that you don't understand. I don't want you to have to change for anyone.

Four is: Realising every year on your birthday that I've learned so much from you and there's so much more to learn.

Exhausted on the couch after the fourth birthday party I said to my husband, 'I'm too tired; my eyes are going to fall out of my head.'

He kissed me on the forehead and said, 'Yep, maybe four is the year of sleep.'

But maybe I *can* take one more year of little visits to my bed.

Little arms around my neck.

One more story.

One more trip up the hill carrying a little boy with tired legs.

I could do this just a little longer to keep you all mine.

Maybe four. Maybe more?

Maybe forever.

Maybe that's what four is?

It's so many, many things.

One thousand four hundred and something days of sleepless nights that you wouldn't swap for pockets full of gold.

A house of flowers, a tired baby, a best friend, lessons learned, a button nose.

Yes, you'll always keep your mama.
As long as you need me I'll be here.

Just one thing: How to calm yourself when parenting is too hard

BY JESSIE MOSS

Jessie Moss is a primary-school teacher, musician, writer, keen runner and Te Reo Māori enthusiast who lives in Newtown, Wellington, with her partner and their two daughters.

This year I have been feeling increasingly paralysed by the seemingly immense and insurmountable list of tasks that surrounds me, from small, everyday parenting tasks and my work as a new entrant teacher, to my role as a partner and friend, and as a member of my community at large.

A Playcentre meeting, lunchboxes, whānau hui, wānanga reo, piles of washing, maths planning, hospital appointments, just one more email . . . and weaving through all of this, the never-ending behavioural and emotional management of small children. This is the grit that threatens to eat into the fabric of the very ropes that bind me together.

As a teacher, I simply put on my professional hat. I take some deep breaths, remember all the theories and best practices I know and I set to work. And I do a pretty good job. But by the end of my working week, I don't have much left in the reserve tank. Over the years, my own daughter, who has ongoing behavioural and learning challenges, has remained a constant but delightful work in progress. This has been exhausting for me.

Our daughter doesn't intend to throw me these curve balls. She doesn't mean to walk my partner and I through these especially muddy territories. She is just getting through life her way. She's just being her. But fuck me, she can be hard to parent sometimes.

So the immense and insurmountable bit is the parenting work. My toddler and my big girl are both doing their best as they are. My work is doing what I know they need. It is being consistent and reasonable and calm. As much as is humanly possible.

When doing these things is difficult, or I know straight up that I'm just not doing them at all, I have two mantras that I bring myself back to:

One thing at a time, and this too shall pass.

Both are commonly known 'encouragements'. They are both simple but they require dedicated effort to enact. The great thing about these nuggets is that I can actually hear the voices of those who originally said them to me: two dear friends, who are also raising wonderful children. So when I think of these encouragements, I can stop myself from spiralling because I can see them seeing me seeing them.

I take a breath.

I regather.

I move on.

I keep to my word.

I am consistent.

There are so many behaviours, inter-sibling warfares and areas of development in our children on which we could focus our parenting at any given time. How do we decide what is most important? Where should that precious energy go? And why is it so hard to unknit all the threads that create these parenting challenges in the first place?

The answer is in the fundamentals of being a child. It all comes back to learning.

Learning is fun for children, and they aren't particularly conscious of doing it. They relish it. The exploration, the attempts and, finally, the mastery of things such as tying laces, putting your reading folder in your bag, riding a bike or making your own breakfast. Some other kinds of learning are not finite, such as social skills and emotional regulation.

We also know children take time to learn — at their own pace, in their own (sweet) time. We know that there is no clear path and no right way to do it. For the often busy adults in their lives, this can obviously be frustrating. And for those of us with kids who walk to a slightly or radically alternative beat — those of us who are supporting children to master everyday tasks and to manage their developing emotional landscapes — this can be really hard, slow and sometimes enraging work.

At any given time, there can be a multitude of objectives, goals, aims, checklists, to-do lists and star charts. We have to juggle all of this stuff. It is possible, however, with practice, to put one thing front and centre, which allows all the other stuff to follow in the slipstream. We pick one focus point, one area of learning that we commit to being purposeful, reflective and consistent about.

For us it is behaviour and emotional management, for them

it is new learning. It is critical that we remind ourselves of this. Children want to do well. They want to please us. They want to learn. It is hard work for everyone, but we are the adults. And they are the children. We have experience and are essentially their life guides. Or sheep dogs, however you want to see it . . .

Consistency is hard. There are so many demands on parents and caregivers that push our limits, that threaten our abilities to be consistent. Strip it back, make it achievable and keep it manageable.

When faced with difficult times, new learning frontiers or changes in our children's lives — I say pick one thing. One thing at a time. Pick the thing that is really driving you the highest up the wall. Put that front and centre, because if you can get that under control, many other things will fall into line, or they might dissolve completely.

And the sense of peace achieved for you and your child will be huge.

It might be that this new learning takes a week, three nights, or a month of dedicated consistency . . . whatever. Commit to it. Be consistent, then move on. To the next one thing. Because this too shall pass. And there is always more work to be done.

Surviving daylight saving when you have kids

BY EMILY WRITES

Days are usually 24 hours, right? Like commonly. Like most of the time. Except after daylight saving. The days after daylight saving — regardless of whether it's September or April — are 850,000 fucking hours long for parents.

For some unknown reason, given that most small children can't tell the damn time, daylight saving is The Actual Worst for parents when it comes to sleep. Why? Why is it so bad? Nobody knows. And there is literally sweet fuck-all you can do about how bad it is.

Put the kids to bed early and they will wake up at 4 a.m. Put the kids to bed late and they will wake up at 4 a.m. Put the kids to bed at their normal time and they will wake up at 4 a.m.

Granted, some people will assure me that their no-routine kid has no issues with daylight saving, but I do not believe this. I don't think you're a liar. Truly. I just have to believe you're full of it or else I will cry forever.

Let's just agree that 99 per cent of us who have kids under four have had no fucking sleep since Sunday. And the other

1 per cent need to shut it and just relish how untired they are. Is untired a word? I DONT CARE.

Anyway, this isn't *just* a rant. I have some tips to help you to cope.

CREATE AN EFFIGY OF GEORGE HUDSON

George Hudson was the bug-loving literal motherfucker who came up with daylight saving (he was also, to our everlasting national shame, a New Zealander). Incredibly, he had one daughter. But, let's face it — he probably made his wife Florence do fucking everything. That's probably why she died well before him — because of all those extra hours she had to fill when she could have been sleeping. Apparently this monumental toolbox wanted *two* hours for daylight saving. Which shows what a massive chode he was.* Thankfully he's dead. He died in 1946. I checked. The hell we endure every April and September is due to Old George wanting to torture insects. So create an effigy of George Hudson. Parade it through the streets. Set it on fire. Howl at the moon.

BE CAREFUL ABOUT SCREEN TIME

There's a reason why you should not use screens too much — and that's because it won't have the zombie effect on your children that you need it to. If you let them watch too much TV it will stop working, and by working I mean that it won't actually silence them at 4.30 a.m. As joyous as it is to watch 16 hours of *Fireman Sam* before you get up and cry in the shower, I recommend switching up screens so your kids don't

---

* I'm sorry if you're a descendant of George's, he probably wasn't a penis.

get too complacent. Give them your phone, then your laptop, then the TV, then the iPad or whatever other devices you have. Chuck on *It* or some other children-getting-eaten horror movie and scare them into silence.

START A CULT AND REFUSE TO HONOUR DAYLIGHT SAVING

Wake up, sheeple! Who says we need to turn back our clocks? What has the man ever done for us? What would happen if we just didn't change to the new time? They can't control us. I mean, they probably can because we're functioning on two hours' sleep a night — but that's what they want, man! That's how they get us. Join me, we're going to meet at 8 p.m. outside the clock tower. Oh, I mean it'll say 9 but I mean 8, OK? Yeah, 8 p.m, 9 p.m. Look, I'll stay the full hour . . .

CHANNEL YOUR INNER PINTEREST MUM

What better way to spend the extra hours you have awake than by filling your Pinterest board? Here's some fridge magnets I made from my tears and leftover soap scum from the bottom of the shower! Make your kids a sensory board with the hopes and dreams you gave up when you had children. Here's a wind chime I made of coins to symbolise my dying career and the empirical evidence of the gender pay-gap in New Zealand.

ENJOY EARLIER BEDTIMES

Some children will go to bed early. Mine were in bed at 5.30 p.m. the first night. Which of course I paid for, because they woke up at 4.30 a.m. But it was nice to have an evening to myself for the first time in a long time. I watched TV and fell asleep on the couch. But you should use this time to go out somewhere or at least think about going somewhere before you realise you haven't seen any friends in years and don't know what anyone else is doing with their lives. Also, send your thoughts and prayers to parents whose children inexplicably go to bed *later* and wake up *earlier* for no reason during the daylight saving war on parents.

GET TO KINDY DROP-OFF/WORK ON TIME FOR THE FIRST TIME IN YOUR LIFE

You did it! Enjoy the one week where this will happen. I mean sure, it'll be the longest work day of your fucking life since you've been up a full eight hours before you even start — but hey! Productivity! Kindy drop-off is a lot more fun when you're there early, so you can make the most of your child screaming at you that they don't want you to go. Cherish every moment!

KNOW THAT THIS WILL HAPPEN ALL OVER AGAIN IN SEPTEMBER, SO YOU MAY AS WELL JUST SUCK IT UP

Why complain? Because it's fun and it makes you feel better, that's why. You thought I was going to end on some nice note here about how much we all love our children and how it's all worth it, didn't you? Well, of course that's true. But also, I'm in it — it's Friday or Wednesday or whatever fucking day it is, and I've been awake for six months or however long it's been since we put the clocks back. So fuck daylight saving. I will write something nice when I'm not so fucking tired.

Rock-a-bye my balls: Why having a vasectomy made me truly appreciate The Wiggles

BY CAMERON LECKEY

Cameron Leckey is a stay-at-home dad who cares for his high-flying wife and two beautiful but completely mad kids. He specialises in dad humour and occasional parenting wisdom.

I love The Wiggles. Whether it's the original Wiggly quartet with their big red car and their 'middle-aged white man' choreography, or Wiggles 2.0 and their more socially acceptable gender balance, inter-wiggly romances and professionally trained dancing, I love them all.

I must confess, though, that the reasons for my love are not entirely pure. Most of their songs are irritating at best, and they've got a fabulous way of getting stuck in your head for days on end. If I had a dollar for every full day that I've spent humming 'hot potato hot potato' I'd be almost as rich as The Wiggles themselves.

No, the reason that I love them is that they are the best and often only means of distracting our children long enough to actually get some shit done. That's right: I freely and wholeheartedly admit that sometimes I use television to distract our children. Judge away, judgy judgicus.

Like pretty much every kid on the planet, our kids are partial to all of the classics. *Finding Nemo*, *The Lion King* and *Frozen* all get some airplay from time to time, but nothing holds their attention as completely as the Wiggles. Car journeys are when they come in handy the most, but I also rely on them from time to time when I simply need a few moments to myself without a little high-pitched voice repeating my name every eight seconds.

But I recently learned to truly appreciate the unique and awesome power of The Wiggles, thanks to my vasectomy.

The procedure itself was so minor that it's hardly worth writing about, except to say that the urologist had the decency to ensure that his hands were warm, there was sport on the television screen on the ceiling (the grown man's equivalent of The Wiggles), and he even paid me a compliment on the spaciousness of my scrotum. He sure knew how to make a guy feel special.

Likewise, the recovery process was far better than expected. I'm pleased to be able to report minimal discomfort, with no swollen purple balls or any of the other horror stories that you hear from time to time, and within a week I was fighting fit again.

The most challenging part of the entire vasectomy process, for me anyway, was the follow-up fertility test. For those who aren't familiar with this part of the process, once everything is back in working order you're expected to fire at least 15 rounds through the barrel before it's safe to assume that the gun isn't loaded any more. Once you've reached this milestone, you then need to deliver a 'sample' back to the lab to make sure that there's no rogue swimmers still bobbing around. Seems so simple, right?

The first problem: the sample has to be delivered to the lab within 45 minutes of deposit. Of course, the labs don't provide an on-site facility, so that means finding somewhere to fill the cup that's within 30 minutes or so of the lab (allowing for parking and a small margin of error). Obviously public areas are off limits unless you want to risk making the sex-offender register. This really only leaves the safety of your own home, which in my case is a 25-minute drive to the lab on a good day.

Then there are the opening hours of the lab. Standard business hours only. Not the ideal time to be doing non-standard business.

But the real challenge, for me, is being a stay-at-home dad with a two-year-old daughter who doesn't let you out of her sight for more than 20 seconds. And that's just not enough time to get the job done — even for me.

So as you can see, the logistics of closing out this vasectomy process and confirming that the urologist's skills extended beyond just a pair of warm hands and some smooth one-liners were proving to be more than a little challenging. And that's where The Wiggles came in. With their help I was able to buy myself enough 'daddy time' to sneak off and get the job done without kid #2's well-intentioned (but highly inappropriate in this instance) company.

We never got to find out who was driving the big red car that day, or whether Jeff actually did wake up, because as soon as the lid was on the special cup I snatched kid #2 away from the television and we were out the door, toot-toot chugga-chugging off to the lab, singing 'Hot Potato' all the way.

So to The Wiggles, both old and current, thank you so much for providing a constant and reliable distraction for my children. Your catchy tunes and colourful performances have once again bought me the time that I needed, and for this I'm deeply appreciative.

Postscript: For the record, kid #2 and I rolled up to the reception area of the lab with minutes to spare. I had sweat dripping off my forehead from the mad dash between my illegally parked car and the lab (carrying kid #2 on one hip). I handed my precious little cup to the receptionist, along with my dignity.

She took her time checking the paperwork was in order, gave the little cup a shake, and somehow, with the straightest of faces, managed to dismiss me with a polite 'Thanks for coming'.

Magic moments

BY EMILY WRITES

When I was pregnant with my second baby, I had a really idealised view of labour. My first labour had been relatively straightforward and in my mind I'd sugar-coated it a lot. Like an absolute shed-load. In my head I'd sneezed and the baby came out. It was nothing like that, as my husband so often pointed out, but I was convinced. Nobody wants to go into labour fearful, so it makes sense that my brain did a wipe-clean and told me it was all going to be a piece of piss.

I decided I wanted a birth photographer, because I was convinced second labours are easier. I'm not a smart person. I know that now.

I have no idea why I thought that. No idea at all. It's based on nothing. But I was convinced. So I saved my pennies and got an amazing photographer. It will come as no surprise that I was wrong and my second labour was horrendous.

And my lovely photographer was there to capture it all. Including the three false starts over two weeks and the very extremely fucking long pushing period.

The first photos I have of my labour are of me looking exhausted and my husband looking bored.

The next lot I have I look more and more like I'm dying. In fact, the photographer made a video of the whole thing that includes me looking up desperately at my midwife after I'd asked if I was going to die. My midwife says in this video, 'You know you are going to have the baby, right?' For some reason I thought I'd just be in labour forever (mainly because I'd been in labour forever).

I spent an extremely long time pushing while my enormous baby ground against my pelvic bone, as he was the wrong way up. So in most of the photos I look like Godzilla about to take out a small village.

All I wanted was that photo that you see everywhere: that photo of a mother who is being handed, or has just been handed, her baby. I wanted that second of joy captured forever. That moment when you become a mother — or when you become a mother again. Getting to that point can be so fraught, I thought by capturing it I could hold the magic in a frame for life.

Through a very talented photographer, I was able to get it. The image shows the agony and the joy and the relief.

If you looked at the photo that captured the moment I held my baby — sweaty but blissfully happy — you might see a beautiful moment, and it is definitely a beautiful moment. But it hides a truth — I was happy not to be pregnant anymore because pregnancy had nearly killed me. I figured the tough part was over. Nothing could be worse than those feelings I had had while pregnant. I knew parenting — I'd had one baby already. I was confident.

When I look at that photo — capturing that precious moment — I look at myself and I think: she didn't know, she had no idea what was coming.

I am completely at peace in this photo. I remember that

feeling so well. I remember thinking everything would be fine now. My baby was here and he was safe. It was all over — we were ready to begin again. There was only light.

We don't know what's coming when we get pregnant. We don't know what pregnancy will be like, even when we have been through it before. We don't know what labour will be like, though we always have expectations.

We definitely don't know what those first two years will be like.

I had no idea that one day I would wake up on the floor of my bathroom and wish I wasn't alive anymore. I had no idea that I'd consider leaving my family — that things would become so desperate that I wouldn't want to be around anymore.

But if I stood before her now, that woman in the photo — holding that cup of tea and her precious baby — I wouldn't say 'Run!'

I'd say this:

Hold fast. Hold tight. Hold on.

You have a world of love that is going to envelop you. You will have the darkest days of your life, but the light will come and it will be brighter than anything you've ever known.

You will survive this, and you will learn that you are stronger than you know.

You will have moments when you feel like you are not a good mother but I promise you, I *promise* you that you will come through this and you will know you are a good mother.

Your marriage will be stronger than ever. Your love will be tested, so tested, but the results will amaze you.

Your wedding day didn't prove your love; what proved it was

the day your husband sat in a ditch with you, convincing you to live, while you sobbed.

This world we live in was born from a universe the size of a golf ball. A huge explosion could have destroyed everything, but instead creation came from it. And all of the beauty you see came from that destruction. Rebuilding is beautiful. You get a new beginning.

She didn't know this.

She didn't know her world was going to be so wonderful.

She didn't know that her dreams were going to come true.

You just can't ever know how beautiful your life is going to be.

So, I'd say to her, as I say to you:

You don't know what's coming, so hold fast, hold tight, hold on.

This is what makes our lives stunning — we don't know what's coming, we can't know, but we can make it through no matter what.

The science of motherhood

BY THALIA KEHOE ROWDEN

Thalia Kehoe Rowden is a former Baptist minister and current mother and development worker. She writes about parenting, social justice and spirituality at Sacraparental.com.

As you carry your sleeping six-year-old back to his own bed at three o'clock in the morning, you hold him close, not just to feel his chest expand and relax, but also to shift his centre of gravity nearer and save your poor back. Physics for real life.

You are a walking nutritional calculator and keep a detailed mental food diary for five people. You know that the toddler has eaten a fortnight's dosage of bananas and rice today, but nothing green. You know that bananas and rice are constipating, so you offer her a couple of prunes as she barrels past, pushing a cardboard-box rocket.

You adjust the five-point harness of the baby capsule, chattering to your rugged-up infant, so as not to think too much about the probable force and angle this cosy armour is designed to shield against. You drive a smidgeon under the speed limit.

You understand the respective and combined properties of sodium bicarbonate and acetic acid, and use them on all manner of stains and grime. When you are cleaning the sink out, you call the children to witness your exploits, shaking baking soda down the drain and slowly adding vinegar. They are delighted, and take your magical knowledge of chemistry for granted.

Your conversation and bearing with these small humans is at the forefront of good clinical psychological practice. You have read up on non-violent communication and do your best to swallow your frustration and impatience, at least most of the time, and instead let your apprentices know how their behaviour makes you feel, and what you would appreciate in the future. You get good at this, because you have a lot of practice.

You know all about the epidemiology of respiratory illness in Aotearoa. You worry, in the winter, about the draughty old villa your children's young bronchial tubes and lungs are living in. You know their bedrooms, at least, need to be warm, and you do running calculations throughout the day of how much power your appliances have used and the current spot price, and reference those figures against your bills account.

You follow friendly scientists on Twitter so you can post pictures of unusual bugs and rocks your kids discover, the ones that aren't in the second-hand identification guides your eight-year-old sometimes sleeps with. You have never known more about the geology of volcanic eruptions, the fate of the dinosaurs or the composition of the solar system than you do now. Occasionally you have the joy of revealing your own knowledge about these things to your children, things they haven't already learned from *Dinosaur Train* or *Wow in the World*.

'Oort cloud,' you say, almost as an incantation, 'Igneous rock.'

You have absorbed more principles of engineering through raising children than you ever did in Year 12 physics. You can correctly estimate, from the kitchen, just how high the two-year-old's tower will get this time before toppling, and you rejoice with her when she learns to construct a wider, more stable base, and her skyscrapers grow taller, just as she does, daily.

You know everyone's height in centimetres and weight in kilograms, so you can calculate dosages of paracetamol, spot op-shop bargains that will fit your kids, and give yourself an inner high-five when you pick the baby up for the seventeenth time that morning, trying to remember not to use your back like a crane. Your biceps have never been more taut.

Your spatial awareness is so well honed that you reach your hand out on the footpath and it finds a small one without effort or thought. You say, 'Looking both ways?' but you know the location and trajectory of every vehicle and hazard in range already.

You can hear breathing from metres away, and analyse it for the last signs of your son's sixth cold this year. Your reflexes are astonishing when tested by an ambitious climber falling off a stool near you, and all the more impressive given your chronic lack of sleep. You may not have eyes in the back of your head, but the two in the front can perceive who is feeling a big feeling, when your daughter needs to be reminded to use the toilet, and who is so focused on building a Lego doll's house that he should be left to it for just a while longer before being called to the bath. You can see these things at the very same time you are chopping vegetables *very finely* to ninja into tonight's dinner.

It has taken longer to develop, but you are now also becoming more familiar with the science of self-care and the skill of being kind to yourself. You are getting better at recognising the skills you bring to the tasks of motherhood, at pacing yourself, prioritising, and judging when to say 'no'. Soon, as well as being an expert in palaeontology, astronomy and mechanics, you will be aware of just how brilliant and amazing you are.

Your children know it already.

The rules of birthday parties for children

BY EMILY WRITES

A few weeks back I hosted my son's fifth birthday party. In my life I've hosted six birthday parties. We didn't give my youngest a birthday party one of the years because I don't know, it's all a blur because we didn't sleep and suddenly we were like oh wow, you had a birthday and we didn't notice. Don't tell him. He's a baby, he won't know.

The last birthday party — the fifth one, the big one — was a dream. My father paid for a disgusting bouncing castle germ-pit that gave a bunch of the kids gastro (but also entertained them for hours). We drank wine while the children played in a fenced-off area. I assume drinking at birthday parties is a no-no, but I felt like I needed a drink to cope with the fact that my tiny baby somehow grew into a five-year-old overnight and my husband almost ran us off the road when I suggested we have a third.

Discussing the topic with other mothers, I've seen there is a real need to nail down the unspoken rules for birthday parties. I figured I would bestow this gift upon the parenting community myself.

The rules are quite simple and I've thought about them

for at least a handful of minutes. Let's break things off into groupings . . .

INVITATIONS

You must invite all of the kids in your child's class or centre or kindy.
Sorry. You have to invite everyone. Because what if one kid misses out? What kind of monster wouldn't invite all 45–75 children in your child's class? Do you want Little Jimmy to be in therapy for the rest of his life because he didn't get an invite to Little Maydeeesynz's birthday? Why did you even have kids?

You must keep the invite list to five kids or less.
Sorry. But you can't invite more than five kids unless you are some kind of climate-change-denying planet-hater. By inviting more children than that, you're encouraging people to have too many children. Do you know we have to have seed farms now? Do you know that? Haven't you seen that documentary?! How do you even have space for more than five children?!?! What is your carbon footprint like?!?! **WHY ARE YOU LIKE THIS?!!?!?!?!?**

Your invite needs to be homemade.
This rampant consumerism needs to stop. Why would you buy a $2 pack of invites when you could spend 20 minutes desperately trying to get your child to make 160 invitations, then give up, then make them yourself while crying and drinking gin straight from the bottle? Why would you, Karen?!

Your invite needs to be made by BabyVitesForeverLove Ltd.
Don't you love your child? Don't you love them as much as RelatableMama87 on Instagram? She has a code for 20 per cent

off, and all the mums are using BabyVitesForeverLove Ltd for their cards. I mean, you don't *have* to use them but I mean . . . why did you have kids if you can't afford them?

FOOD

You need to have organic wholemeal gluten-free paleo quinoa oil.
Some parents want to kill their children with sugar. If they just did some research they would see how *dangerous* sugar is. What kind of mother gives their child cheerios? Mother Bates? Mrs Eleanor Iselin played by Oscar-nominated Angela Lansbury in the landmark 1962 thriller *The Manchurian Candidate*? Fairy bread? Why don't you just serve them bees holding knives? **LETS JUST SMOKE CRACK** — you're halfway there if you're going to serve Twisties. Honestly, organic wholemeal gluten-free paleo quinoa-oil-based kale grain-free artisan chips are easy to source if you care about your children enough to spend longer than three seconds preparing for their birthday party.

You need to have cheerios and fairy bread.
Why do children's birthday parties need to have healthy food? Why can't our children just enjoy themselves?! **CAN'T THEY HAVE A CHILDHOOD?!?!** Why are you depriving them of sugar?! Why do you hate them!? Why did you even have them?! I can't stand sanctimummies and their obsessive sugar obsessions — what are you, Kate McCallister of *Home Alone* and *Home Alone 2* leaving your child at the airport or something? Just let them eat cheerios and fairy bread, you monster! In my day we just gave them a bag of cane sugar and they just ate it and they were happy. Not like mothers today. **ALWAYS MAKING A FUCKING FUSS.**

CAKE

You need to make your cake at home.
You need to make your child a homemade cake. I mean, it's not hard. I made my children an exact, full-size, anatomically correct *Mister Maker* cake. I collected all of his measurements off Tinder. It took only 160 days, a two-month course on fondant, and a small piece of my soul but it was worth it. Because I love my child. No judgement, friend.

You need to buy your cake.
What is this shit? Buy a cake that looks good — your appalling attempt at the train from the *Australian Women's Weekly Children's Birthday Cake Book* reminds me of the 1946 Hunan rail disaster. Jesus, Karen, get your fucking shit together.

THE PRESENTS

Insist on no presents over $8.25.
Stipulate the amount all presents must be worth. I believe $8.25 is the perfect amount. Ask for receipts and if any mother goes over this amount, cast her into playgroup oblivion. Put a photo of her face at the entrance to all cafés and insist she cannot be served.

Insist on 'no toys'.
Do you know a seal ate a My Little Pony and it got excluded from the colony and now it lives in my bathtub? Don't put that on me, Karen. Don't make me have to adopt all these fucking half-plastic sea animals. If you give children plastic toys, you hate dolphins. Why do you hate dolphins? What the hell is wrong with you!? You shouldn't be allowed around children.

Insist on charity donations instead of presents.
Excuse me, my children don't want presents because they care about charity. Look, we all spend, what, $15,000 each when we buy a birthday present for a party. We go to, what, 150 birthdays a year. Add that up over six years! We could have $64,000 to give to the Everyone Needs A Custom-Made Handbag To Match Their Mountain Buggy Foundation. Make sure you bring a receipt, you cheapskate — I'm going to check to make sure you actually gave money to the Ponsonby Shih Tzu Rescue Alliance.

Don't you dare put the interests of your child on the invite to helpfully give us an idea of what they might like for their birthday.
It's really cool that you think I'm made of money and can afford to buy a *Star Wars* battleship Lego Play-Doh castle. Little Soriasis has more fucking shoes than I do and literally everything she could ever fucking want and now I have to buy her an Elsa That Pees too?

Present or no present is fine.
What am I, a fucking wizard? Tell me what is socially acceptable. Do I let my child pick a present based on what they think your child will like or do I get away with not doing anything? Is this going to bite me in the ass somehow? Don't ostracise me. Please. I need this.

Handmade presents only please.
Yeah, cos I had nothing better to do than to make your child a fucking origami orangutan while I try to get off watching old episodes of *Sons of Anarchy*.

GOODIE BAGS

Now, this is controversial. It's just important that you know that you need goodie bags. But also do not have goodie bags.

OTHER EXTREMELY EXTREMELY IMPORTANT RULES

* You can leave your child at the party if they're over the age of 308 months.

* You can bring more than one child if the invite says you can bring more than one child.

* You can bring more than one child if you have more than one child.

* You cannot bring more than one child if you have more than one child.

* If you are going to the birthday of twins you need to get them a gift each.

* If you are going to the birthday of triplets you need to get a gift each for the first two but not for the last one, to create a healthy rivalry.

* If you are going to the birthday of quads you need to get just one gift and make them fight for it.

* You need to bring baking — but don't go to any trouble. NB: two days of baking isn't trouble.

* Please leave your husband who talks too much at home.

* Your au pair can only come if she's less attractive than me.

* Every child gets a turn at Pass the Parcel or you're never allowed to host a birthday ever again.

* Excuse me, piñatas are cultural appropriation and they encourage violence.

I hope you've figured out by now that this is a joke. It has taken me a while to realise you can't do a birthday 'the right way'. It will always be 'wrong' to someone. But all that matters is that your child is happy.

After my son's fifth birthday, which I went all-out for, I asked him if it was his best birthday ever (don't judge me — I wanted validation from him). He said 'It was my second almost best birthday.' Before I could say **WHAT THE FLIPPIN' HECK. CHILD**, he continued: 'My best birthday was your own one birthday when we got our nails all done nice and we had cakes and teas.'

For my thirtieth birthday we'd had a high tea and then, even though I had bitten my nails down to nothing, I let my son pick nail polish for me and we got manicures. I still remember the beautician looking at my nails like, 'Woman, get on some anti-anxiety medication.' I guess I forgot how much my son loved that day. All I remember was that my boobs hurt and I was exhausted. To him, though, it was special because it was just the two of us, having some time together. It was a reminder that the little things matter just as much as the big stuff, and we can't lose sight of that.

Birthdays are a way for us to celebrate every sleepless night, every giggle and joyous moment. It's also a way to mark that you got through the tough stuff, too. For us, five signalled something really special — we still have our baby, when others who were in the children's ward with us don't. So many parents lost in the pain of infertility or miscarriage would love to struggle through the politics of just one birthday. Others mark birthdays with tears as they no longer have their baby with them. Not every birthday is guaranteed for children or their parents.

So do rules matter? No, I don't think so.

Maybe the one rule we really need is just gratitude. No matter what we do, we must do it with a thankful heart.

I'm not babysitting and mums are getting a raw deal: A dad on gender roles in parenting

BY BRANNAVAN GNANALINGAM

Brannavan Gnanalingam was born in Colombo, Sri Lanka, in 1983 and is a writer and reviewer based in Wellington. His fifth novel, Sodden Downstream, *was published in 2017, and was shortlisted for the 2018 Ockham New Zealand Book Awards.*

You know, things would be pretty sweet if our own incompetence was celebrated. Imagine every mistake at your day-job being comedy gold — 'Haha, Brannavan, he's so shit, what a joker, good one, Brannavan'. Yet there is one job where incompetence is still turned into everyday comedic gold. And that's being a parent. Or, rather, a male parent.

Obviously this doesn't apply to mothers. Mums are expected to lean in and be the perfect Type A while pretending to be a Type B genius in everything they do, including parenting. For dads, our starting level is set at 'incompetent'. Many people are surprised if we do much more than 10 per cent of parenting duties.

Now, I'm a pretty happy-go-lucky fellow. There's a reason why I've had a stomach bug in every inhabited continent in the world (except for North America for some reason), and that's because I am, for the most part, an 'it'll be all right' kind of person. When it came to most baby-related things, I had no idea what I was doing in the early days. I still don't, really. I hadn't seen a nappy since I was toilet trained (excluding that one time we did that prank in high school involving Marmite). I would have watched a YouTube video about how to put one on, but I was worried about what the authorities might think of my search history.

I didn't realise the first time I did the baby bath by myself that I should have had the towels and change of clothes ready before the bath. As the only vegetarian in the house, my sneaky attempts to propagandise vegetarianism via lentils backfired 12 hours (give or take) later. I probably should have learned how the car seat worked before I tried to put a baby in it for the first time, coming home from the hospital. And did you know babies needed to nap?

But how many mothers know their shit before a baby is born? Unless you're the oldest child and your parents were strict Catholics, most of my new-mother friends had little to no idea what they were doing either.

But boy, was I given a lot of rope. I couldn't imagine a mother getting that sort of leniency. A baby crying in a restaurant? You, mother, you're as annoying as that time I ate pizza too quickly and burned the roof of my mouth. How dare your baby cry on the plane when I'm trying to get drunk by myself because it's one time drinking alone isn't judged but actually encouraged? God, why are you taking 20 minutes to strap your kid into the car seat while I'm waiting here blocking one entire lane of rush-hour traffic because I'd really like your car park?

When I'm looking after the child by myself, I'm 'babysitting'. Now, if I was a teenager earning sub-minimum-wage and drinking a bottle of vodka on the sly, then maybe I'd be a babysitter. Otherwise, it's called being a parent. 'Daddy Daycare' is apparently what my home turns into the moment my wife steps out of the house. I'd love to run a daycare. It'd play D.A.F.'s 'Der Mussolini' on repeat while the kids were forced to practise their slip catching, and parents would pay me in solid gold and overseas holidays. My home, though? Nah, it's child-proofed, kinda, and features three square meals a day.

'Ooh, your wife is having a night out? How will you cope?' Dunno: the same way that I've managed to take care of myself the majority of my adult life except those times that I got those stomach bugs.

When I've had to leave early from something to do my parenting duties, I'm frequently treated as if I'm not rushing home to anything particularly important. My criticism of the patronising concept of 'dad duties' isn't, however, an open invitation. Dads, keep your own babies in your own respective houses.

If there's one thing this world doesn't need more of, it's a guy talking about how to be a mother. But bear with me. It strikes me that there are two ways to ease the pressure on mothers to be perfect. 1) We *all* get to be incompetent, regardless of assigned gender roles. Or, at the very least, the fact that none of us knows what the hell we're doing isn't seen as that bad a thing. 2) Dads everywhere could up their game: for starters, learn to cook, clean, bathe, change and hang out with their child. Jokes about incompetent dads need to become as unfunny as your mate when he's drunk too much and is provoking a fight with a random stranger for no real reason and you're all looking at your shoes.

I suppose the answer's a combination of both: lowering the expectations for mothers and raising the expectations for fathers. If society has an expectation that children will be raised perfectly but that half the parents get a free pass to be half-arsed, it's not particularly realistic to put all of that burden of perfection on the other half. And, if your dice as a dad is that you want to pretend to be some ten-year-old boy who just needs to be mothered when confronted with a baby? Dude, I hope you're not taking care of my aeroplane or providing for safer communities together or defending me on my criminal charges or whatever it is you think manly men should be doing instead.

'Are you Nana?' and other tales of older motherhood

BY JANE BRIGHT

Jane Bright is a writer, editor, musician and proud mum of two amazing daughters.

I had my first daughter a couple of months before my thirty-seventh birthday. Until my kids came along, I was pretty ambivalent about pregnancy and motherhood. But at 36, I decided that, uncertain as I was about the whole business, I'd better get cracking, as much to see what would happen as anything else. Having read the same hand-wringing articles as everyone else about the dangers of 'leaving it too late' — the creeping, punitive infertility that inevitably afflicts the older would-be mum — I found myself, much to my surprise, knocked up in a matter of months. Phew, I thought. That was easy. Honestly, I don't know what all the fuss was about.

I lie. Actually what I mostly thought was:

Why is it called morning sickness, when it should really be known as All The Livelong Day Sickness?

And: Oh God. I'm going to be sick. Again.

We were living in the UK at the time. Twenty weeks into an uneventful — if vomit-splattered — pregnancy, I presented myself at the local NHS hospital for the second scan. At the 12-week scan, we'd been entranced by the sight of our little peanut pinging his/her way around my uterus, and I was looking forward to finding out whether he/she had mastered the barrel roll.

Instead, the scan complete, we were ushered into a dimly lit side room, and plied with tea and explanatory pamphlets. The scan had detected an anomaly: the umbilical cord, apparently, is supposed to have two arteries and one vein, but it seemed that I'd inadvertently opted for the cut-price version with just the one artery. This was thought, at the time, to be associated with neural-tube defects such as spina bifida or anencephaly. To see whether our baby was affected, an amniocentesis was recommended. This would involve inserting a long needle into my belly through to the uterus and drawing out a sample of the amniotic fluid for analysis. It carried a small risk of miscarriage.

'What should I do?' I asked the midwife tearfully.

'That's a decision only you and your husband can make,' she replied, kindly but unhelpfully. We walked home in silence. On the way, I stopped at a toy shop and bought a wooden pull-along snake for my baby. As much as anything, it was a gesture of defiance.

The obstetrician we saw the following week had no reservations about offering his advice. After examining the scan and consulting my notes, he reassured us that the baby looked developmentally normal and that the cord abnormality was probably just an anomaly. In fact, the risk of miscarriage from the amniocentesis was considerably greater than the likelihood of the baby having a neural-tube defect. 'Go home and enjoy your pregnancy,' he added firmly, showing us to the door. He wore a blue and white spotty bow tie; I felt reassured and, for the first and only time in my life, grateful to a man for telling me what to do with my body.

I went home and, while I didn't actually enjoy my pregnancy, I didn't dread its outcome quite as much as I had before the encounter with Dr Bowtie. My daughter was born — well, not so much born as evicted — by caesarean, 12 days overdue and thoroughly healthy.

My parents visited from New Zealand when she was three months old. It was a difficult time: I was trying to conceal the postnatal depression (PND) I was convincing myself I didn't have by keeping an immaculate house, cooking full, nutritious meals from scratch, and refusing help of any kind. My parents didn't know quite how to respond to this, and spent most of the visit sitting bolt upright side by side on the sofa in terrified silence. When the baby cried, my father joked that they had 'packed the fish slice' — the utensil used to discipline me and my siblings as children. (Later, in bed, I would rage and weep to my husband about this remark.) On the last day, as they headed out to the taxi to the airport, my mother laid a hand on my arm and looked into my eyes. 'We're so glad you didn't have a handicapped baby,' she said. 'Because you're not exactly a spring chicken, you know.'

In my strung-out state, this observation left me reeling. I was heartbroken, and furious. With myself, as much as with her: it was my fault for caving in and telling her, for not keeping my damn fool mouth shut. I shouldn't have rung her in tears after the scan (but before the consultation with Dr Bowtie).

I had this coming. And if I'd had a 'handicapped' baby, it would clearly have been my fault — a punishment for my ambivalence, for telling my mother about the scan, for daring to try to have a baby as an older mother. My beautiful, healthy, vociferous daughter was something I had got away with; something I clearly didn't deserve. Next time (although at this stage I couldn't even contemplate a Next Time) I might not be so lucky.

(Months later a compassionate young GP finally got me to admit that I was, in fact, desperately depressed. It took him three consultations over two days. In the end, he managed to convince me to start taking Prozac, and after that I felt much better. Eventually.)

We moved back to New Zealand to be closer to family, whereupon my husband began the campaign for Baby Number Two. My initial reaction was 'Are you fucking kidding — I'm not going through all that again', followed by a litany of what 'all that' had entailed: month after month of vomiting, a long and difficult induced birth culminating in an emergency caesarean, enlivened by a post-partum haemorrhage and followed by a blood transfusion, my agonising and short-lived attempts to breastfeed, and of course the PND for good measure.

Clearly I was not good at this, I didn't believe that I was going to improve with practice and what's more, it was downright unreasonable of him to expect me to try. And then there was the little matter of increased risk factors, for everything: birth defects, miscarriage, stillbirth, maternal death. Even if he managed to defy statistics by knocking me up, I would be almost 40 by the time the baby was born. Shouldn't we just be grateful to have one healthy baby, and not push our luck?

My mother-in-law offered to pay for a private consultation with an obstetrician to discuss my misgivings, especially in light of the scare we'd had the last time. Naturally, I accepted this kind gesture gratefully and with grace.

I lie. I am a stubborn bastard, completely incapable of accepting help where it is offered, so I muttered a terse refusal and decided to tough it out on my own. And I went ahead and said yes to my husband, yes to another baby. Because it was something that was in my power to give him. Because he looked so heartbroken when I said I wasn't sure whether I could do this again. Because, watching our daughter in the playground, I realised that I didn't want her to go through life playing by herself.

I weaned myself off the Prozac and we got to work. Once again, my attitude to the whole process could only charitably be described as ambivalent. I even issued a caveat: if my husband didn't manage to impregnate me by the time I hit 40, we would be stopping at one kid and that was that and he would just have to lump it. But no pressure. Much to my surprise, again, I fell pregnant in a matter of months.

My mother-in-law expressed her joy at my unexpected state by bringing me flowers and, for some reason, an electric wok. My mother's reaction when I rang her was, 'Oh, you brave girl', which I decided to take as an expression of approval rather than a caution. (At least it was better than the spring chicken comment.) Our second daughter was born by caesarean at 39 weeks, just after my fortieth birthday.

Now aged 10, she is the healthiest child I have ever known, so healthy that recently our family doctors sent us a letter querying whether we still wanted her enrolled at their practice, since they hadn't seen her for three years and she was about to be deregistered.

I'm the first to admit that I got lucky. Incredibly lucky. But I have no deep or inspiring thoughts to offer on whether motherhood is more fulfilling later in life because you are more mature, more grounded, more sure of who you are, partly because I don't think any of those things describes me, and partly because I have no experience of young motherhood with which to compare it. In fact, I often wonder whether motherhood is best undertaken when you are young and resilient and energetic, and still think nothing can touch you.

One thing I can tell you that is not fulfilling about older motherhood is being asked 'Are you Nana?' (so far, by a relief teacher at my daughter's school, a checkout operator at Countdown, and at least two of the well-meaning retired ladies who pour the tea at mother and baby groups — not that I'm keeping count). I have yet to come up with an appropriately withering response. Then there's that awkward moment while making small talk about family when you mention your kids' ages and a fleeting expression of ill-concealed astonishment reveals that the other person had assumed that your children were grown up, possibly with children of their own. At playgroups, being visibly 20 years older than some of the other mums can also make you feel a little self-conscious. And going through menopause at the same time your daughter is going through puberty can hardly be described as fulfilling — although simultaneously navigating a private hormonal blizzard of my own does offer a salutary reminder of what the poor child's going through.

As to work-life balance, all I can say is the impact of a late career break is much heavier when it takes place before your career has really taken off, all the more so if you decide to have children when the ink's barely dry on your dissertation. After nearly 14 years of juggling part-time and freelance work around being my children's primary caregiver, I have now accepted that my career's well and truly on the skids. And as I watch women more focused and less diffident than me combine family life with high-flying careers, I'm especially conscious of how far I fall short of the popular image of the older mother as a mature, well-established woman of substance. Meanwhile, I'm still trying to figure out what to do with my life.

All of this comes back, of course, to the fear of being judged. As mothers, we're often made to feel that however we're doing it, we're doing it wrong, especially by choosing to 'delay' motherhood. But I didn't choose older motherhood — it just happened that way. I didn't meet my husband until I was in my late twenties, when I was just about to embark on a Masters followed by a PhD overseas. I had it all worked out. Only once I'd finished the PhD did I even start to contemplate having a baby. And if the term 'biological clock' refers to some overwhelming emotional imperative, I can't say that I've ever heard any ticking. Having a baby just seemed like a good idea at the time.

And in the end, none of this matters. I can truly say that my kids are the best thing that's ever happened to me. I feel incredibly lucky that they are both smart, funny and kind and, most importantly, healthy and happy. I can't imagine life without them. They are who they are because of who and where they came from. I wouldn't have it any other way.

A parenting glossary

BY EMILY WRITES

When you become a parent it feels like you enter a whole new world and in that world the language is different. You promise yourself you'll tell your child things once (and once only) and then suddenly it's 'If I've told you once I've told you a thousand times' and 'Don't make me say it again!' and 'What did I say??' and really 'What did I just say?'

Here's a glossary to help you on your journey (I'll only say it once).

Alexander Skarsgård Eye candy when the days have been too long.
Antenatal group Hopefully they'll become your best friends and will hold your hand through this crazy parenting journey.
Aoooof If you have a male partner, this is the sound he will make the first time the baby accidentally punches him in the balls.
Bath water Preferred drink of choice for toddlers.
Black poo When you first open a nappy and you're like, what in God's name? That's meconium. You'll be told about it. But you need to see it to believe it.
Car seat Your baby will view their car seat as either the best place in the world or the worst place in the world. There is no in between.

Code brown   A child always shits in the public pool. You can only hope it isn't your turn.

Coffee group   The place where everyone claims their child is sleeping through the night but trust me — their child is not sleeping through the night.

Cot   A great place to fill with laundry while your baby sleeps on top of you.

Day three   Three days after delivery you will have a clash of hormones so epic you will likely lose all ability to control your emotions in any way. I became convinced my husband was leaving me because I couldn't work the coffee machine.

Declaration of independence   I DO IT!

Floor food   Nine toddlers out of ten prefer 'floor food', the breakfast of champions.

Fournado   The level of destruction a four-year-old can do in five minutes while your back is turned is a sight to behold. This is called a fournado.

'Gentle hands!'   Repeated six to 976,473 times a day for a year while your baby learns not to pull your hair/pull the cat's tail/punch their sibling in the face.

Grandma's house   Heaven.

Hairy Maclary   The Sacred Texts.

Hot coffee   Now you have cold coffee.

Instagram   Your house will never be as clean as hers. And she's not that happy.

Nipples   Will become the size of dinner plates and handle the most intense pain imaginable.

Pants   Your child will go through a stage where they see pants as a cruel and unusual punishment.

Pelvic floor   You used to have one.

Peppa Pig   Your co-parent.

Poonami   Usually babies make sure poonamis happen in public or as soon as you get in the car. They'll likely involve poo from ankle to neck, and will coincide with you forgetting wipes.

Shoes For some reason your child will see shoes as torture devices.

Sleep That thing you once had.

STOP! What you'll yell as your child makes a run for it in the public toilet when you're mid-pee.

The second night The first night you feel smug because your baby has only woken up to blink at you and gaze adoringly at you. The second night they will likely realise they're not in a nice, warm place and they will loudly, ear-piercingly protest this fact. You can't put them back in.

Threenager When you think 'Why do they call them terrible twos — they weren't that bad!' And then your child turns three and says NO to everything.

Whisper fighting When you need to yell at your partner but you can't wake the baby.

Wipes The things you need most in your nappy bag that you will keep forgetting to put in your nappy bag.

Pull your weight: If there's two of you, you both need to parent

BY JAI BREITNAUER

Jai Breitnauer has worked as a writer and editor for 18 years, and her passions include parenting, health, sustainability and vegan food. She lives in Auckland with her architect husband and two ballet-mad boys, one of whom has additional needs.

Long, long ago, in a hemisphere far, far away, there was a little girl called Jaime who liked red ribbons in her hair, grapes in her lunchbox and horse riding at the weekend. Every morning after a breakfast served by her mum, she would hop in the car with her dad, who would drop her at school on his way to work. When the school bell rang at 3 p.m., Jaime and her friend would gallop like horses out the gate to meet their mums, in a sea of mums.

At home, Jaime and Mum would do homework before Mum

drove Jaime to swimming, or Brownies, or ballet. Back home around 6.30 p.m. Dad would come in, ta-da! like the hero father from *The Tiger Who Came To Tea*, and they would all sit down to dinner — except Mum, who would be up and down fetching things for Jaime and Dad. After dinner, Jaime's mum would read her a book and sing her to sleep in her beautifully tidy room that Jaime felt sure wasn't tidy that morning.

When Jaime got older she realised a few things:

* Mum did actually work. So did many other mums, often in under-paid jobs like cleaning and admin, so they could fit work around their children.

* Mum worked two jobs. When her part-time paid job finished, her other job preparing meals, doing laundry, cleaning, helping with school projects and being a taxi began. That made her working day much longer than Dad's, which finished at 5 p.m. followed by a bath and a beer and Brucie on the telly. This second, unpaid job is referred to by sociologists as the 'second shift'.

* It's unlikely there was a real tiger in *The Tiger Who Came To Tea*. The mum was probably just fed up and created an elaborate ruse to go out for a feed.

So, Jaime became Jai, got some qualifications and a good job, and set her sights on an egalitarian relationship. She met a lovely bloke called Noah who was adamant he wanted to be a hands-on father when they had kids.

As luck would have it, Noah got to put his money where his mouth was, due to being made redundant two weeks before baby number one was born. We entered this new Bohemia where we both freelanced and whoever had the work had the desk, and the other one had the baby. It was wonderful, even though there was no guarantee of getting paid, and often we both had work at the same time. In those cases we had to learn to share a chair while balancing the baby on our heads.

Then baby number two came along and, briefly, Noah got a 'proper job' with a salary, and a car, and a tie, and we were all miserable until I said: 'Stuff this, I want to be the editor of a magazine.' So, I did that for a bit, and he joined Playcentre and generally brought some energy and creativity back into daily life. Eventually, though, we realised what we both wanted was to 'have it all'.

A lot has been written about whether women can 'have it all', and pretty much everything written about that woefully neglects the fact that many men don't either. They don't even get close. Because having it all means having a good chunk of everything — including the 'second shift'. For us both to have it all we had to share the load, 50/50, even the shit neither of us wanted to do.

I went to a great public lecture recently called Engaging with Dads, jointly presented by three fab organisations, Great Fathers, Family Success Matters and Father and Child. Aimed primarily at social workers and those involved in supporting vulnerable children and families, it was a real eye-opener in terms of the importance of fatherly involvement if you're parenting with a father or father figure. It relates to one-mother, one-father families.

Dave Owens from Great Fathers noted that children who had involved dads from day one usually have much better outcomes in later life. They're better at making friends, better at problem solving, secure enough to explore the world and their place in it, better able to cope with frustration and control aggression . . . Key, I thought, in a nation where one in three women experience family violence, was that boys with involved dads were less likely to be violent as adults. Boys and girls with involved dads were less likely to experience teen pregnancy, substance abuse, end up in jail or be at risk of suicide.

Owens referred to this as 'The Father Effect', and pointed out that waiting until your kid is nine and taking them to the park for a kick around isn't the same as being an involved father. He noted that when dads hold their babies, their bodies are subject to a physical, hormonal response just like women's bodies are, and that response causes permanent positive change in the babies' brains.

David Ringrose from Family Success Matters noted how important it is to engage men, especially fathers in vulnerable families, early on. He noted how little trust some of these men have in social workers and government agencies. They've been let down, and they need to be met on their own terms. They need their confidence rebuilt and for their friends and family to see how capable they are.

Brendon Smith from the Father and Child Trust said that studies show a high percentage of dads are not actively involved in their child's life. The result is that many fathers are forgotten in services for parents. He said he has met with staff at a local agency who said, 'Our policy is we don't have to ask if there is a dad involved.' Brendon noted that mental health, development and poverty outcomes are usually better for children with an involved dad.

He noted that postnatal mental health issues affect dads too, plus women with PND have faster recovery times and better outcomes when the dad is involved. Multiple studies, he says, have shown that a happy relationship, with both parents taking joint responsibility for the child, leads to better outcomes for the child. So important is this fact, it is a tenet of law — the UN Convention on the Rights of the Child (UNROC), ratified by the New Zealand Government, states that governments should support fathers and mothers as a child's right. Yet when Smith contacted UNROC to ask what changes could be made to enable this, he got no response.

One thing that Owens said that resonated with me was the idea of a 'maternal gateway'. There is a subconscious presumption in our society that men are incapable of taking on 'maternal' responsibilities, and so it should all fall to mum. This stereotype has persisted in popular culture with, for example, those memes about 'what happens when you leave Dad alone with baby'. Funny as they are, they devalue a man's role at home, and the sad thing is that this myth is often perpetuated by men themselves.

This infantilising of grown men really is the sharp end of shared care, and something I can't support. People have asked me, 'How does your husband get the kids to sleep when you are working away from home?' or 'Do you have to leave meals and instructions for him?' and my answer is no, because he's a fucking adult. I don't thank my husband for doing jobs and taking the load off me, I thank him because we are a team, and team members support each other.

Our day usually involves Dad dropping the kids off at school before heading into the office. I work from home, so I will do a load of washing or run a quick errand in my breaks. Four days a week I pick the kids up from school, and on one day, my husband does the deed. Crucially (and if you have a willy and a sense of entitlement this section is definitely for you), the four nights that my husband doesn't pick the boys up from school doesn't mean he wanders on home when he fancies, cracks open a stubbie and asks what time dinner will be served.

We appreciate that evenings are also shared-care time, and that means we share responsibilities at home while supporting each other to have personal interests.

It really does take a fucking village and we are lucky to enjoy the support of great friends. On top of that, our various employers and clients also actively support our family goals, offering flexibility and understanding that our children are a priority. While we know plenty of people who share care, as well as those people who choose to stick with traditional roles (and I salute you! After all, feminism is about having choices), there are also those who would like to share care but cannot because their husband earns more, or because their family does not approve, or because they just don't have the support of their workplace and/or social connections. Often, it's the people at the lower end of the socio-economic spectrum, who need this flexibility and support the most, who don't receive it.

We are a Straight, White, Affluent Family (SWAF — I just made that up, cool, eh?) and that means we have options that aren't always open to other types of family. Yet supporting the choices of men and women underpins the notion of equity — and equity is the key to scaffolding our children effectively, raising good citizens and in turn lowering family-violence rates and improving mental-health outcomes.

Inclusion of both parents in the hands-on raising of a child or children is a total no-brainer. And yet we still have employers refusing flexi-time, we still have healthcare professionals focusing heavily on mums rather than dads, and the primary eligibility for paid parental leave still lies with the mum, with paid parental leave possible for dads only if the mum transfers it to them.

Enabling shared care of children by both parents should be a priority for the government, but it requires big legislative, industry and social change — otherwise for many, it's simply not an option. The change is simple. When you place the child at the centre of the support system — as recommended by the UN — inclusion of both parents becomes logical. I for one would like to see New Zealand leading in this area, but for now my watch must end — it's my turn to pick up the tamariki, and we have big, big plans for today.

My baby slept through the night six times so now I'm an expert on getting your kid to do that

BY EMILY WRITES

For the last almost two years, my son has been exceptionally committed to never sleeping. It wasn't just that he woke many, many times a night. He also didn't have naps during the day, woke exceptionally early and found it difficult to go to sleep at night. So some might say I don't know shit about child sleep.

But actually, in the last month he has slept through the night four times. So now I am a qualified sleep consultant.

Here's my excellent advice on how to get your child to sleep through, based on the six times in two years my son has slept through the night.

ROUTINES

We have a strict routine — dinner, book, bath, bed. We have adjusted the time we put him down by half an hour over the last year or so.

Here's what I know: three of the times my son slept through the night were after we followed the routine to the letter. The other three times the routine went out the window and he slept through the night. So I would recommend having a routine or not having a routine.

WHITE NOISE

We used white noise two of the times he slept through the night, so white noise might work for you. Or it might not, because all of the other times it didn't work. But do you count from the times he slept through or not?

MAYBE BE ON A BOAT

The first time he ever slept through the night we were on a ship in a cyclone. So, you know, see what you can do about that.

CO-SLEEPING

Co-sleeping has saved our sanity 100 per cent of the time we have co-slept. It has also made me lose my will to live after being kicked in the kidney and screamed at and farted on 100 per cent of the time. So I would recommend doing it or not doing it 100 per cent of the time.

DRUGS

Sleeping pills have helped me sleep through the night. You're not allowed to give kids sleeping pills. I checked.

NOT BEING ON WAKE-UP DUTY

Five of the six times he has slept through, my husband has been on duty, which is grossly unfair and a great injustice.

NOT HAVING ANYTHING PLANNED THAT NIGHT

If you want to go out because it's your anniversary, your child will not go to bed. If you have too much wine, pretending you're 18 again, your child will wake up 56 billion times. If you have a bad sleep, that'll be the night your child wakes so often you feel like you're entering the pit of hell when you walk into their room. For some reason, if you fall asleep watching TV your child will sleep through the night.

FLOOR BED

The floor bed worked four out of six times! Lots of room to stretch out. It also might not work, because he had a floor bed for ages and it didn't work. And then it did work like six months later. Almost like sleep is a developmental milestone . . . hmmm.

SINGING 'STAIRWAY TO HEAVEN' IN MONOTONE

Definitely helped because that song puts everyone to sleep.

ALWAYS PUTTING THEM BACK IN THE COT

Did not work ever. If your child doesn't want to sleep in the cot, they're not going to. Burn the cot. Smash it with an axe. Actually, donate it to charity — don't scare your neighbours. They have to put up with crying all the time (you and the baby), and they had to deal with that time that you stood outside in labour screaming at your husband to 'PACK THE FUCKING BAG IT IS COMING OUT I AM NOT HAVING THIS BABY ON THE FUCKING DRIVEWAY AHUUUUUUUUURRRRRGHHHHHHHHHHHH' (weirdly specific). Or the time right after that when you screamed 'MY VAGINA IS BURNING IS THAT THE HEAD IS THAT THE HEAD?' (also, quite specific — adapt as needed for your situation).

JUST ASKING THEM TO GO TO SLEEP

Totally works. LOL no it doesn't. Fuck that noise. Who gives this advice? Like honestly. Of all of the advice, this is the worst.

COMPLETE SILENCE

Often necessary. Heaps of noise also works. So either quiet, silence, noisy, loud — one of those things might work. You could maybe try all of them and just see. Once a fart upstairs woke up my baby downstairs, and then on Guy Fawkes Night he slept for like four hours in a row. He also slept through an hour-long flight including take-off and landing, despite the fact that me breathing wakes him up at home.

ACCEPTANCE THAT SLEEP IS A DEVELOPMENTAL MILESTONE AND YOUR CHILD WILL JUST SLEEP WHEN THEY CAN AND THEY'RE NOT OUT TO UPSET YOU. THEY'RE JUST BEING A BABY AND THIS IS WHAT BABIES DO AND IT SUCKS SO HARD BUT HONESTLY, THEY WILL SLEEP THROUGH ONE DAY. I PROMISE

This is the best advice you can take. Really. And it sucks that there is no magic bullet. No spell to be cast. This is it. Babies are all different. Some are good sleepers and some are bad ones. And the ones who sleep just sleep — there isn't a trick. You're not doing anything wrong by ignoring advice that doesn't feel safe or respectful.

You're not a bad parent because your child doesn't sleep. You don't need to do things that feel wrong just to 'teach' them to sleep. In my experience of having a child that *never* sleeps I can honestly tell you that babies will sleep when they sleep. It's that awful and simple.

It is so bad, honestly, I know. But we did nothing differently with our son. There's no reason why. No sleep aid that changed anything. No point where we knew why it has been the way it has been. He has just started to turn a corner. He does not sleep every night. But one night helps us through one week. He can do it, and he'll do it again.

It will be the same for you. One day, your baby will sleep. And you will sleep. I promise. And when you're in it, it just feels like that doesn't matter. Because right here, right now you're exhausted beyond measure. I know that.

But I promise you, when you start to see the light without a sleep-deprivation headache thudding away, this feels revolutionary. Nothing you did caused this. Your baby isn't bad. There's no reason for this. It was just luck. A spinning wheel that landed on No Sleep For You. It'll all change soon. I promise. Until then, you're not alone.

Will I remember this?

BY EMILY WRITES

I'm greedy to keep all of the moments of my child's childhood. He is always running. He jumps from foot to foot and I can't slow him down. He can't stop moving.

Every day there are new gems, new words that make my heart swell, all tumbling out and disappearing as soon as they hit the air. I try to fold them like they're precious letters and stow them away. I try to file the words away in my mind. I snatch pieces of paper and write 'Bonocoly' because what will I do if I forget that his favourite game to play with his dad was Bonocoly not Monopoly?

What if I forget all of the things his dad says to him on the baby monitor? Like when he lost his beloved teddy bear and was told: 'Look mate, part of being a dad is not losing your kids. It's actually probably the most important part of being a dad. It's actually really the only thing. You need to keep an eye on your kids and make sure they don't get lost.'

I don't want to remember the sleepless nights and the whispered fights, but I do want to remember the time we were discussing how to solve our latest parenting conundrum and my tired husband said: 'It doesn't work at all. But you know, we should keep trying it' before we dissolved into laughter over our wine.

I can always conjure up the image of my husband standing at the door of our babies' room — smiling as they sleep. Will that always be the case?

Will I remember trying to distract Eddie while he had an IV line put in? When he whispered: 'Will they take all my blood?' with fear in his squeaky voice. 'Will they leave some for me?'

I reassured him and asked 'Would you like to be a nurse or a doctor when you grow up, Eddie?' He looked shyly at those holding his tiny hand. 'No thank you,' he said.

'Well, what do you want to be?'

'A dad. I want to be just like my dad.'

Today, Eddie said he had a gift for me. Princess drink from a plastic cup.

'Drink it,' he said smirking.

I raised the empty cup to my lips and a horrified look flashed across his face.

'I sorry Mama!' he yelled and pulled the cup from my hand.

'What?' I asked him.

He hung his head in shame.

'I farted in the cup so you would drink my farts,' he whispered.

OK, maybe I don't need to remember everything.

Screen time isn't the enemy

BY ANGELA CUMING

Angela Cuming is a print and radio journalist. She has three boys under three and hasn't slept in five years.

Opinions about kids using iPads are a little bit like the toys you get inside Kinder Surprises — everyone who has anything to do with children has one rattling around somewhere, and they are all pretty bloody annoying.

This week yet another childhood 'expert' popped up to tell me I am a terrible parent for giving my kid an iPad to watch stuff on. 'The iPad is a far bigger threat than anyone realises', the headline screamed.

The author retold a story — that I am convinced is actually a Parenting Urban Myth — about being in the checkout line at a supermarket and watching a kid go absolutely nuts (probably wanting a Kinder Surprise) before the frazzled mum handed them an iPad to keep them quiet. This apparently will lead to all sorts of negative things such as obesity, depression, aggression, poor social skills and, most horrifying, the reluctance of children to run around outside and build 'dens' (I assume she means something other than the opium kind).

Sigh.

It's hard to know where to begin, but maybe it should be at the point where we let go of this ridiculous idea that giving your toddler-on-the-verge-of-an-epic-public-meltdown your iPhone so you can get them, and the shopping, in the car, is wrong. It's the point where we recognise that a five-year-old watching YouTube isn't going to use their screen time to watch snuff movies or old footage of Charles Manson and run off to San Fransisco to join a cult or the Republican Party.

It's the point where we say, you know what, it's OK to let your kid sit like a zombie on the couch for an hour or more because it keeps them calm and happy, and lets Mum or Dad get the three other kids fed and bathed and dressed in the pyjamas and **WHY DO WE EVEN HAVE TO JUSTIFY THIS?**

Take my three boys. I have two-year-old twins, Tommy and Henry, and a threenager, Charlie. I have an old iPhone that I let Charlie use to watch stuff on YouTube. And there's absolutely nothing wrong with that. It doesn't make me a bad mum, or a lazy mum, it just makes me a mum.

Charlie loves it. He has a thing for the original *Thunderbirds* series, so I search for old episodes and he watches them, clutching his little *Thunderbirds* vehicles and re-enacting the rescue scenes. He watches that godawful annoying yet reassuringly educational Blippi, and now asks about things like apple picking and snow ploughs and aquariums and other such horrible, dangerous stuff.

I give him the iPhone when he's feeling sick and sleepy and needs to rest in bed, or when I am knee-deep in twins and need a chunk of time to get dinner sorted and laundry folded, or when Charlie's a bit overwhelmed by a big day and needs a bit of downtime in his bedroom by himself. We sometimes watch it together, huddled under a duvet and gazing at NASA rocket launches, pretending we are in outer space.

And here's the thing. Charlie is a bright, engaged, funny and active little boy, and the only potential negative to ever come from his screen time is that he now knows the difference between a front-end loader and a backhoe. And woe betide anyone who gets those two toys mixed up when you are drafted in to help him build his road in the pile of sand he's swept up in the backyard.

We need to stop shaming parents for letting their kids watch what are effectively tiny little television screens (and I bet 50 years ago, mums were being shamed for letting their kids watch too much TV). It's fine, they won't have stunted speech or form square eyes or turn into zombies who rock themselves to sleep or scream hysterically for hours on end and think Blippi is their real mummy.

You are not creating bad habits by giving your child your iPhone to stop them losing their shit in the supermarket; you are parenting, and doing a bloody great job of it.

The iPhone or iPad is not the enemy. It's a great tool for firing a child's imagination and teaching them new things and for exploring the little known world of people who make videos of themselves unwrapping different novelty chocolate eggs (it's a thing).

And besides, once the kids are done with YouTube you can always pour yourself a wine, kick back on the couch and use your screen time to search for photos of Justin Trudeau when he was in college. You're welcome.

Surviving Wine Mum Night

BY EMILY WRITES

It's Wine Mum Night! It's taken eight weeks to organise this night. Husbands, wives, boyfriends, girlfriends, grandparents, flatmates — whoever it is, somebody else is watching the kids. You worked around birthday parties and sick kids and work, paid and unpaid, appreciated and ignored. The village has stepped in.

It's a proper night out.

I'm talking the sort of night where once you get home you don't have to wake up to the kids all night *and* you get to sleep in — it feels like you have to make the most of it. It's your forever night. It has to sustain you for months, maybe even years. Forever.

You need this. You've been knee-deep in poo and spew, toilet training, not sleeping ever, cooking, cleaning, dealing with everyone's crap. You need a break.

Which is why we have Wine Mum Night. And it's a sight to behold.

Chances are either you don't drink often because your kids never sleep, so you live with what feels like a permanent hangover, or you've been pregnant and/or breastfeeding. Which means: lightweight. So here's an anatomy of a Wine Mum Night (I know, because I've had a few in my time — in fact, though it's not obvious at all, some of this post is based on my own experiences . . .).

5.30 p.m. — Oh, the pressure! You can't wear your maternity leggings. You *definitely* can't wear your breastfeeding bra. The kids have long since claimed all of your jewellery and the teething necklace you wear every day looks like anal beads.

But you're so keen to leave the house and flee your children/responsibilities that you don't take longer than 15 seconds to get ready. The look you're going for is Kristen Stewart's MILF sister, but you look more like your almost 65-year-old uncle who insists he toured with the Grateful Dead.

6 p.m. —You meet the girls. You left early to skip the bedtime routine. If you'd stayed you would have been stuck lying by the cot for two hours and then you'd be too tired to leave the house. This is how you missed Wine Mum Night last time.

6.05 p.m. —You have a moment of silence for your comrades who couldn't make it because their child got sick, they got caught in the bedtime routine, they fell asleep at 5 p.m., or their husband is a massive turd and you're going to spend all night verbally destroying him and plotting how you're going to split them up.

6.10 p.m. —You all agree that nobody can get drunk because we all have the kids the next day and nobody can cope with hangovers.

6.20 p.m. — Shots of absinthe for everyone.

6.30 p.m. — The Circle of Judgement begins. You plan revenge on one of the kids who is hassling your child at daycare. Insist no baby is ugly before agreeing that yes, that particular baby is unfortunate looking. Eviscerate your boss/partner/frenemy/Karen who stopped us being able to drink at school committee meetings. Her kid was sleeping through the night from six weeks old. What a bitch. She's lying. Definitely lying. Bitch.

6.31 p.m. — 'It's so bad how mums judge each other! I never judge! We need to always be kind!'

6.45 p.m. — Agree it is boring to talk about our children who we love very much/are driving us to drink. More pinot gris. One friend suggests you all buy drugs and then says JUST JOKING but you know she's serious.

6.50 p.m. — Everyone is drunk. You take your Spanx off in the bathroom and put them in your handbag.

7 p.m. — Nobody has any money. How does wine cost $15 a glass now? Half of the group is gawking at the group of tradies who just walked in — not because they want to get them into bed, but because they're thinking they look so tall, and will all of our baby boys grow up and become tradies? What will they look like? Will they get married? Will they give us grandchildren???

7.05 p.m. — Everyone compares c-section scars and loudly talks about their pelvic floor and how many Kegels they can do. You tell the bartender what a mucous plug is.

7.15 p.m. — 'I'm so gay!' 'We know.'

7.20 p.m. — Everyone agrees we should all live on a commune together with no men. We can all be sister wives and we'll raise our children together. There is lots of crying and hugging as we all agree we are best friends forever.

7.30 p.m. — Shall we buy some cigarettes? Oh my God, they literally cost $100 now. Everyone smokes while insisting they don't smoke.

7.45 p.m. — 'YOU ARE SUCH A GOOD MUM LISTEN TO ME YOU ARE SUCH A GOOD MUM . . .'

7.55 p.m. — *Screams All Saints *Never Ever* in monotone*

8 p.m. — Men are the worst. We should kill them all and rip

their still-beating hearts from their bodies.

8.01 p.m. — I love my husband/boyfriend too! I don't know what I'd do without him! OMG, I'm going to call him!

8.20 p.m. — IS THAT BEYONCE?! OMG I LOVE HER!

8.22 p.m. — It's not a broken ankle, it's fine. Wow, is that the bone? Hmmm, maybe my bones are always a bit poky-out-of-skinny LOL.

8.30 p.m — 'My back has just been really bad because the baby weighs like 18 kg now, it's insane?!' *pulls out phone* 'Look at these 6000 photos I took this morning.' 'How old?' 'Oh, he's 54 months old now.'

8.45 p.m. — I'm so tired. I shouldn't drink anymore.

8.46 p.m. — Just a pinot gris please. No, a bottle.

8.55 p.m. — The bar cuts you off. The bartender tells you that you've reminded him he needs to call his mum.

9 p.m. — You need a kebab. You tell the guy making your kebab your birth story.

9.14 p.m. — You fall asleep with one shoe on, cradling a kebab.

9.15 p.m. — You get home.

5 a.m. — You wake to the sound of your kids, with the worst hangover you've ever had in your entire life. Your children reward you for having a night out by screaming at the top of their lungs for two and a half hours straight. One of them climbs into your bed just to piss in it. You go back to sleep in the wee. Your partner comes in every five seconds to ask, 'Where are the nappies?'

10 a.m. — You enter the vortex of hell, AKA Chipmunks. You eat 10 chicken nuggets then throw up in the ball pit and blame it on a child.

11 a.m. — There is no 11a.m. There is only pain.

11.05 a.m. — You swear you're done with big nights out. Then six months later. . .

Duking it out with my partner over whose life is harder

BY SARAH MITCHELL

Sarah Mitchell is a stay-at-home-mum, recovering ex-lawyer, traveller and life adventurer, with a lifelong love of reading and writing.

I am currently competing in a long-running, intense and hard-fought contest. My foe is my partner and co-parent, and we compete over which of us has the hardest, most exhausting and least fun life, now that we are parents.

I'm pretty confident that most couples with young children are engaged in this same battle over whose life is the crappiest, day after day, year after year.

Our child is a typical toddler. A sunny, joyful, charming wee dot. She delights us every day with the new and wonderful things she says and does. She has brought so much pure love into our lives and is truly the best thing that has happened to either of us. She can also be an emotionally volatile, demanding, nonsensical, never-shuts-up, tiny tyrant. We are typical parents of a toddler: we both adore our child and crave occasional time away from family life. So, in the evenings, each of us presents our case for why our day has been the most terrible. The winner of this debate receives the most child-free time, a break from the everyday grind.

A typical conversation might go like this:

Partner: How was your day, darling? [as I pass him the flailing toddler]

Me: Oh, suuuuperb. Would you like to hear the stats? It involved one ripped library book, one lost set of keys, followed by one refusal to get in the car seat and consequently one missed coffee date, one refused nap (including independent removal of a pooey nappy), one dinner thrown on the floor in disgust, two full-on tantrums (including one at the supermarket with 10 spectators), and five million deep breaths inhaled by me in order to not lose my shite entirely.

Partner: Oh, I'm sorry about that. I had demanding colleagues, unreasonable clients and a bus that was 20 minutes late. I have a call at 8 p.m. tonight and another at 6 a.m. tomorrow and I haven't prepped for either.

Then we stare each other down, thinking: your day was soooo not as hard as mine, you wimp!

I remember an actual conversation we had recently. I had been cleaning mould out of our basement for approximately 6000 hours, removing and washing MDF shelving (never, I repeat *never*, use MDF in a room prone to dampness). My partner had been occupying our toddler while I undertook this task. When our gorgeous darling woke from her nap, my partner asked me if I was going to get her up, since I'd had the morning 'off'.

I replied (using my best downtrodden housewife voice and

face): 'Ummmmm, I've been de-moulding our basement. It hasn't exactly been a party fun time for me. Can I please just finish the job? Then I'll come up.'

He agreed (with only a barely detectable huff) and left. Normally, evicting fungal creatures from a cave-like room is not my activity of choice on a sunny Sunday. However, in this case, I gave myself an inward fist pump, popped my ear buds in and relaxed back into the delicious combination of brainless chore and fascinating podcast, with only a smidgen of guilt.

The problem with the Crappy Life contest is the absence of an independent arbiter. It is impossible for either party to believe that the other has it worse. As the stay-at-home parent, I am wholly unsympathetic to some of my partner's complaints. 'I can't believe I have to go out for work drinks again this week!' (Of course — I would much rather be negotiating the witching hour than downing French champagne and having adult conversation.)

Or, even less convincing: 'I am really not looking forward to that work trip . . .' (Of course — I too would dread 14 hours of uninterrupted media consumption on an international flight, followed by seven nights of eight hours sleep, alone, in a king-size hotel bed). Pull the other one, buddy. Likewise, on the days when he finds out that I spent naptime re-watching Jon Snow's sex scene for the tenth time, my partner probably questions whether I'm really as exhausted as I claim to be.

Please don't misunderstand me: I love spending time with my daughter. However, sometimes when I think about my life now, I don't recognise myself in it. The person I am today is so entirely different from the person I was pre-child. Of course, I miss nice things like sleep-ins, having docile brunches at peaceful cafés whilst browsing the Saturday paper, and being able to take a shower without someone pointing at my crotch and laughing. But what I really miss is the feeling of having no real responsibilities. The freedom to leave my job and go travelling for a year on a whim (which I never did, but hey), to move countries or just do anything outside of my house during the hours of 1 and 2.30 p.m.

All major life changes hurt, but this transition, from the relative freedom of early adulthood to the back-breaking obligation of parenthood, is the most painful change I've experienced. And it's ongoing. I anticipate that it will take years to accept that my life has transformed irreversibly and that I will never be the same person again.

Having time away helps. If I can put aside my responsibilities for 30 minutes while I have a (hot) coffee, for a morning while I go for a bush walk, or for a weekend while I get off-my-tits drunk with my girlfriends, I can return to 'real life' feeling refreshed and ready to take on the challenges that caring for my beautiful little monster presents.

Even more desired is having my partner acknowledge, or at least just stare blankly at me while I explain, that my life is unfathomably harder than his. That I have given up more freedom, more fun, more sanity than he has, in pursuit of our joint dream to have a family. When I whinge about my day, I definitely hope for some free time, but what I really seek to win is the (questionable) glory of being the owner of the suckiest life, the legitimate claim to the iron throne of self-pity. I want the dubious joy of having a metaphorical neon sign pointing to me that says: 'Of the two of us, her life is the most crap and it's all my fault'.

Above all else, I want him to hear and understand that I am in mourning for the freedom of my former life, even though I wouldn't give up my current one for anything in the world.

He does hear and understand me. He sympathises wholeheartedly, because he is going through exactly the same grieving process. We are both slowly recognising that we have entered a new season in our lives, as all people who are lucky enough to live such lives do, many times over.

Knowing that this transition is acknowledged and shared by my partner makes it easier to accept, easier to move on from each crappy incident, so that I can appreciate the beautiful, wonderful and precious parenting moments that go hand in hand with the tough ones.

So, I will happily retain my seat as the Queen of Crap Land, grateful to have a King of Crap Land sitting by my side, sharing the trials, tribulations and unprecedented joys of parenthood with me.

Actually, make that the Duke of Crap Land.

Terrible and great crowdsourced hacks to make you feel better about your adequate parenting

BY THE SPINOFF PARENTS

Need a parenting hack? These brainwaves are courtesy of contributors to Spinoff Parents. Note: don't necessarily try these at home . . .

* I bribe my child to behave in public so often that we've worked out how to do it through hand-squeezes. Three hand-squeezes means 'Shut up, you'll get a McFlurry on the way home.' It's perfect, cos people think I'm squeezing her hand to be reassuring and because I'm a loving, devoted mother. Somebody once picked up on it and I

said it stood for 'I love you.' She genuinely thought my love for my child calmed her down.

* For the 40-Hour Famine we sponsor our kid not to talk for 40 hours.

* Pretend to time your kids to get them to bring you stuff. See if they can beat their fake previous record.

* Laundry washing power mixed with hot water gets the smell of spew out of carpet and fabric couches and is way cheaper than fancy, useless cleaning products

* If they have a favourite soft toy, get an identical one so you have a spare. But make sure you swap them from time to time so the spare isn't suspiciously clean.

* When I don't want to play with my kids, I pretend to time them doing circuits of the playground. They leave my side for minutes at a time.

* Before you get the Lego out, spread a sheet or blanket on the floor and tell the kids they *must* keep it all on there. Then at pick-up time you just roll up the sheet and pour it into the Lego container and it's so much quicker.

* Don't put your vacuum cleaner away, and leave it on at all times. Eventually all the crap on the floor will get shovelled near it and the sound will help drown out your whining child(ren). (You're welcome.)

* When they are little and won't eat something, give the

illusion of choice. When my son refuses food, instead of offering him one piece I'll present him with three of the same pieces of food and he picks one and eats it.

* When your kid eats red paint, encourage them to eat blue or green paint as well. It's less concerning when they shit purple than red.

* Buy all of the same colour socks — or all of the same pattern — so you don't have to match socks any more.

* Lay down garbage bags underneath a fitted sheet, because mattress protectors are expensive and kids piss the bed all the time.

* When my threenager is feral at night and won't go to bed even though he's tired, I put the clock forward and trick him into thinking it's midnight. He thinks at midnight he turns into a pumpkin.

* I tell my kids that monsters live in rooms that are messy but they hate clean rooms.

* Put snacks (raisins, popcorn, etc.) in plastic bottles. Should buy enough time for a good, private poo.

* I put pens and pencils into a DVD case for trips. And I take the Peppa Pig DVD, smash it into a trillion pieces and then set it on fire for my mental health.

* Give your baby banana so when they shit in the shower it's easier to pick it up in one go.

* I taught my kids a game called 'Little Fishes' — they have to be really, really quiet little fishes for as long as possible or a great white shark (me) will eat them. It gives me 20 minutes at a time to contemplate why I had so many children.

* Turn the pram into the sun; it makes the baby shut their eyes.

* Use a syringe for Pamol, antibiotics, etc. That way, when they're screaming, you just squirt it at the back of their mouth and they get such a shock and are so outraged that they stop screaming and swallow the medicine.

* Thank everyone who gives your kid a present, but keep the terrible noise-making toys in a cupboard as gifts for other kids' birthdays.

* Layer up clothes, partially for warmth but also cos you only really need to change the top layer of clothing, and only then if it's got dirty at kindy or it's bedtime. The under layers are fine for a couple of days, so long as a nappy doesn't leak.

* Refer to chippies as 'crackers', so when your kids ask for them in front of other people your kids sound like they don't eat junk food.

* Socks work just as well as mittens.

I'm sorry I white-washed your world: A letter to my Māori daughter

BY NICHOLE BROWN

Nichole Brown is a single mother to Emmy. She is Ngāti Porou and Ngāti Hine. She homeschools and travels the world with her daughter writing about her experiences.

To my sweet little girl,

I am so sorry for white-washing your world.

I am so sorry for not giving you a name that reflects who we are. I love your name — it fits your face perfectly, and when it falls from my lips I know that it is you, but I am sorry for not giving you another name, even somewhere in the middle, that gives your name more meaning and depth. A name that reflects your heritage, the language that our elders speak, and the mighty women who paved the way before you.

I am so sorry that it took me until we decided to leave this beautiful country to realise just how important our culture is to our future. I never considered that the Māori legends explaining how Māui fished up Te Ika A Māui for us, and how he caught the sun, would be anything more than stories in a tattered old book — until I realised that these would no longer be the stories you were taught.

I am so sorry that it has taken me four and a half years to take you to stand under the mahau on the front steps of your own marae, to walk through the old carved waharoa made from hand-cut timber, and to gaze upon the wall of our tūpuna.

I am so sorry for calling them 'koomrah' and 'paawiz', when they are kūmara and pāua. I should have taken you to the secret little spring below Grandma's whare to pick watercress for our kai, instead of buying it in little zip-locked plastic bags.

I am so sorry for saying I took you to Towel-Poe and Towel-Wrong-Uh and Row-Tah-Roo-Uh, when we had been to Taupō and Tauranga and Rotorua. I thought they sounded better when I said them so savagely and bitterly incorrect, butchering such beautiful names with my ignorance.

I am so sorry that you had to learn the colours and numbers in te reo from your kindy teachers instead of from me. I was proud of you — tears in my eyes proud — when you started at tahi and ended seamlessly at tekau, but I still wasn't ready to be proud of myself for all of the repressed words that came flooding back to my voice.

I am so sorry for never taking the time to learn my pepeha, and for not being able to tell you yours. I didn't think it meant anything to me — it just felt like a cluster of words and phrases that talked about insignificant streams, mountains and areas.

I didn't feel its power until I saw you dip your little hand into our awa — and then I knew.

I am so sorry that the stick game played with newspapers bound by coloured tape is lost on you, and that you don't know the sound of the rhythm. Yet. I feel stripped bare by the knowledge that we have never sung 'E Rere Taku Poi' together, swinging poi stuffed with old pillows, and with four-plaited tails.

I am so sorry that I couldn't see the beauty of our lands until your innocent eyes gazed in utter amazement at the treasures our whānau holds. You look at our little marae nestled safely under the watchful shadow of the rocky cliffs so steeped in history, in the exact same way I look at you.

Thank you, my little wise one, for showing me life through your new eyes.

Thank you for encouraging me to kōrero Māori with you. Hearing the words flowing flawlessly from your lips makes me catch my own blunt words every time. I'm tempted to fall back into poor pronunciation and half-strung sentences. If you can pronounce Tāwhirimātea after hearing his name once, I know I can say Kaikohe instead of Ky-Kowie. When you yawn, 'Mōrena, Māmā' through heavy lidded eyes and a lingering stretch each morning, I know I can reply, 'Mōrena, pēpi, kei te pēhia koe?' without feeling ashamed of my own mother's preferred tongue.

Thank you for diving into the folds of whānau life — the respect you instinctively give all the tamariki on the marae by calling them 'cousin', the respect you give any of the slightly greying by calling them 'papa' or 'nanny', and the respect you give anyone in between by calling them 'auntie' and 'uncle' without being taught tells me that your heart knows that while family is you and I, whānau extends to everyone who comes through the doors of our wharekai.

Thank you for showing your appreciation of the humble ways our people have lived and thrived — for getting out and picking pūhā, for making games out of collecting fallen fruit and scooping them into a net you made with the bottom of your jumper, and for being brave enough to try smoked tuna. Even bedtime on a mattress in a wharenui filled with snores is met with your smile and innocent excitement. You make me remember that we are blessed to have a wharenui all of our very own, that bears the name of my own Māmā.

All this has renewed memories and traditions for me, and even though every bit of this is new for you, you belong right here in this beautiful bilingual and heavily historical world.

Our roots are something to be proud of. Our stories are begging to be told. Our lands, our marae, and our taonga are to be treasured. Our language is precious. Our traditions are beautiful.

Our history belongs in our future.

Our roots run deep.

We are connected to these lands, to Papatūānuku, to Ranginui by both sun and by moonlight, to the bounty of Tangaroa, and to the wind song of Tāwhirimātea, bound together by the embrace of Tāne Māhuta.

Te reo is more than just a language — it is an art, a piece of our history, and one of the few living connections we have to generations past. A pepeha is more than just words — it is a summation of how we are connected to every living and non-living part of the earth, and the feeling of this connection is indescribable.

I lost my way. In a world I painted white, I lost my way.

But we're here now, and you have shown me the beauty in the world I so desperately tried to forget. And now I will do anything to shine a light on your love for our culture, and to feed your thirst for our language, and to uphold tikanga Māori as best we can together.

He ātaahua te reo Māori.
He whakamīharo mō tātou tikanga
Ko Aotearoa taku manawa.

How to survive the school holidays

BY EMILY WRITES

I said to my husband earlier in the week, 'These school holidays are unending!' and he said, 'Emily, it's 10 a.m. on the first day. Are you drinking wine in a mug?'. It was in that moment that I realised 1) I needed a bigger mug and 2) I should definitely write about school holidays since I'm clearly so good at them.

So with that in mind, I've spent a whole 15 minutes or so coming up with amazing ideas to help you survive those two weeks of enforced joyous compulsory family time. Let's go.

PLAY THE 'GRASS IS GREENER' GAME

While your children watch 1600 hours of *Paw Patrol*, scroll through the Facebook pages of your friends who don't have kids. Oh look — she's just come back from Ibiza and bought a house. She has three pug dogs and her own business. Hide in the toilet so your children can't hear you crying. She's going to Paris for a vow renewal with her husband. Your husband taught the kids to fart in their hand and now they keep coming up to you and blowing fart residue in your face. CLOSE YOUR EYES AND IMAGINE PARIS.

TELL YOUR KIDS TO PRETEND THEY'RE DOGS

Put leads on them and walk them to the dog park. Once you're there, take their leads off and make them run until they fall asleep. Bedtimes are so much easier when you lock them in a crate. Tell the mums in that judgy Facebook group that you've been doing 'imaginary play' throughout the holidays.

TAKE THEM FOR A VISIT TO THE LOCAL NURSING HOME

Old people love kids because they've forgotten what they're like. Let the kids tear around the rest home and watch the old people try to deal with it. If they get upset, say, 'I thought you said in your day you knew how to parent. Go on then: parent.'

TELL THEM ABOUT GLOBAL WARMING

Take them to the beach and show them all the ways a penguin can choke to death on bits of rubbish if they're not mauled by dogs. Explain the Paris Agreement, anti-intellectualism and the Age of Trump. They'll be so afraid for their future they'll be nice and cuddly and nearly catatonic for the rest of the day.

TAKE YOUR CHILDREN TO CHIPMUNKS AND SEE IF THEY SURVIVE THE TERROR THAT IS CHIPMUNKS DURING THE SCHOOL HOLIDAYS

Prepare them with knee and elbow pads and a helmet. I find that giving them a pep talk before I send them in helps: 'This is your one shot. Stand your ground. I believe in your ability to vanquish your enemies and reach the promised land (of the ball pit). Fight and you may die but you will look back on this moment knowing you stood against great odds. Wounds heal, power is forever.'

Eat chicken nuggets in peace.

Remember, if you leave your child in the ball pit, the Chipmunks staff will raise them as their own. I had a third child once. Thanks, Chipmunks!

CELEBRATE ONCE YOU'RE HALFWAY THERE

You've made it through one week, so chances are you will make it through another week. Do not think about the Christmas holidays looming ahead, where you will have a soul-destroying 150 weeks with your beloved children at a time when nobody has any money because they need it for travelling and buying stupid shit nobody wants. The July holidays are actually the easiest holidays as they're only 20,160 minutes long. Take a deep breath — you're almost there. This is a marathon and you're nearing the finish line, and hopefully you're not going to be that person who shits themselves and turns into a meme.

TAKE THEM TO TE PAPA AND SPEND 14 HOURS LOOKING AT THE GIANT SQUID

My son used to think the squid was sleeping because I am soft and I wrap my children in cotton wool, meaning they will probably live with me for all of eternity. So every time we visited Squiddy (why hasn't Te Papa named him?), my son would say, 'Oh, he's not awake! What a shame. One day he will be awake.' Then on one fateful day an old man turned around and said to my angelic child, 'He's actually dead, he's been dead a long time.' So I punched him in the face and used his walking frame to finish the job. What kind of asshole tells a baby that a squid is dead? 'He's sleeping too,' I said to my son and the children surrounding the man's body. 'Just like the squid.'

SPEND 45 MINUTES TRYING TO STOP YOUR CHILD FROM RUNNING IN THE WATER AT THE BEACH

It's two degrees but take your kids to the beach anyway. Spend the whole time trying to stop them running into the water. They'll get their socks and shoes wet and it will be miserable and you'll yell in front of another family and be sweaty and stressed out. But you'll get to post a photo on Facebook afterwards proving you have wonderful family time on the beach with your wonderful family.

GO TO THE ZOO AND TRY TO STOP YOUR TODDLER FROM SCREAMING IN THE KIWI ENCLOSURE

I live in fear that one of the kiwi will die because of my toddler's shrieking and I'll end up on the front page of the *Dominion Post* as a kiwi killer. All my toddler wants to do is go into the kiwi enclosure. I clamp my hand over his mouth and tell him that the kiwi will eat his face if he makes a noise, but he still screams with excitement when he sees it. Kiwi must hate kids so much. I bet they're distraught that they can't fly and therefore can't peck the shit out of noisy toddlers.

SPEND $50 TAKING YOUR FAMILY TO SEE A MOVIE AND HAVE TO LEAVE HALFWAY THROUGH BECAUSE ONE OF YOUR KIDS IS SCARED/BORED/PISSED THEMSELVES

Why are kids' movies so long anyway? Why was *Cars 3* eight hours long? It makes no sense. Nobody needs that much time to tell a story. Especially when the story is just car wins race eventually. Movies are too long, and *Peppa Pig* is only like five minutes. Thank God for the people who make Peppa marathons on YouTube. The 336-hour one is just the right length for school holidays. Also, be prepared for at least one meltdown when your child spills their popcorn one point five seconds after you bought it and gets upset because the superhero movie is not for children, for some inexplicable reason.

SIT IN THE FAECAL MATTER AT THE PUBLIC POOL

Who doesn't enjoy a warm urine soup to sit in? Code browns are as common as unidentified matter in the shower drain at the public pools. School holidays in the spray pool are a time for floaters, and we all know our own child's turds are easier to handle than someone else's. Watch the poor underpaid pool staff deal with crap — for once in your life it's not you handling it. What could be better?

START UP A SMALL CRACK FACTORY IN YOUR SHED SO YOU CAN AFFORD SCHOOL-HOLIDAY PROGRAMMES

Your boss won't let you have a day off because we live in a capitalist nightmare. You get the honour of paying $80 a day for some sixth former who is probably as high as a kite to sit and paint rocks with 100 other kids for four hours while you try to complete eight hours work in that time.

GO ON A HOLIDAY!

Have just as much stress as you always have but in a new environment. Look at the beach through the window as you do endless dishes because the bach doesn't have a dishwasher. Spend most of your time trying to stop the baby burning themselves on the fire. Spend the small amount of money you have on a holiday that seemed far more relaxing in your head than it is in reality. Listen to the kids say 'I'm bored' and 'I want to go home' over and over and over and over again. What's more fun than flying with children? Your child getting an ear infection five minutes into the holiday and screaming for the entire plane ride while a woman getting a connecting flight to Ibiza glares at you. Don't look at me like that, Karen — your dogs have breathing problems.

WRITE PASSIVE-AGGRESSIVE COMMENTS ON FACEBOOK ABOUT HOW MUCH YOU LOVE THE SCHOOL HOLIDAYS

May I suggest, 'I love my children so I spend every second of the school holidays aching with a fulfilment so agonising it's almost unbelievable.' Spread some low-key insults based on your particular situation. For example, 'I don't abandon my children for work so school holidays are just a continuation of joy and wonder for me.' Or, 'I actually work an actual real job so school holidays are so satisfying it's almost vulgar.' Or, 'I love every millisecond with my children — why would you even have children if you weren't going to make it your life's work to surgically create a pocket in your stomach flesh for them to live in for all of eternity?' Try to add, 'They're only young once, you'll miss this time together' wherever possible, and caption all Instagram photos with #schoolholidaymagic #teamworkmakesthedreamwork #sunshineeveryday #sohappyishitmyself #sofuckinghappyicouldfuckingdie #ourloveisasbigasthisdeadbloatedwhalewefoundonthebeach

ENJOY YOUR CHILDREN

Cherish every moment, for in less than a minute your children will be fully grown adults and you will be in a rest home dealing with a bunch of asshole parents bringing their asshole kids into your space. Watch the little brats run around and think: 'These parents are unbelievable. In my day, I loved the school holidays! The school holidays were for family. We enjoyed every second, cherished every moment, and were so blessed it was physically painful.'

The Masterbatorium: A queer experience of conceiving

BY DR WYNTER BRISCOE

Dr Wynter Briscoe is a social scientist with a special interest in gender, although she mostly uses her qualification for arguing on the internet. She works for a small not-for-profit organisation wrangling people, stories and data. She and her wife live in Wellington with their son and an enthusiastic beagle named Lovegood.

Content warning: This post talks about fertility and conception and may be upsetting to couples who are trying to conceive.

For years we referred to our bathroom as 'The Masterbatorium'. We were a house of women who liked showers and baths very much, but the naming came from what happened in our bathroom once a month for six months.

A very generous, wonderful male friend, and his very generous, wonderful female partner, would come around to our house. We would put on some music, they would go into the bathroom, and we would go as far away as possible while still being on the property. A little while later they would emerge with sperm. In a container. For us.

The first time they came around I'm quite convinced we were all various shades of tomato red. It was possibly the most awkward conversation I've ever had. That includes the one where my great uncle intimated that he knew the woman I was travelling with was 'you know' and ended with a literal wink and nudge. You don't know how much your friends love you until they cope with a conversation about the best kind of music for them to jerk off to. In the Masterbatorium. It needed to be something loud, that put them both in the mood, but not too much in the mood. Faith No More was perfect, although I still can't listen to 'Falling to Pieces' without getting anxious and giggly.

The first time, I bought the biggest syringe I could find. I was sure a turkey baster (while traditional in the movies) would be unhygienic, but they're not exactly small kitchen utensils. I waited outside the chemist with all the people wanting to swap needles at 8.57 a.m. on a Saturday morning.

So when our donor's wife handed over the container I nearly said 'Is that all there is?' I'd been conditioned by the 'wet spot' conversation and stuff in books about the difficulties of swallowing. I'd never had 'sexual relations' with a man, in a Clintonesque or other manner. I thought a 20ml syringe would be required. Not so much.

We were so careful that first time. After much thought and

many discussions my partner was the one trying to get pregnant. She'd given up beer and coffee and submitted to me taking her temperature and asking invasive questions about mucus and mood. We thought it would be nice to have sex as part of our baby's conception and to dilate the cervix through orgasm. But we weren't quite sure of the science involved and there was all this advice about keeping your legs up the wall for 20 minutes and how quickly you needed to squirt the strange-smelling spunk stuff in. Plus the embarrassment factor of having just said goodbye to friends who'd christened our bathroom in a very particular way. I can't say it was romantic.

We did it another eight times. Five months in we started doing it twice a month with a day in between each insemination, because science suggested it might help. Our faces weren't as full of blushes. I bought a ten-pack of 5ml syringes and the container was pretty much anything plastic we could find and recycle. We had to change up the Faith No More for some Queen (avoiding 'Fat Bottomed Girls'). As our friends left we'd manage to meet each other's eyes and talk about the telly. Once they stayed and chatted to our flatmate. Sometimes after they'd gone we'd have sex; occasionally we'd talk politics, sometimes I'd read Harry Potter aloud.

I'm pretty sure the day it worked I abandoned her to cook dinner after 10 minutes of her legs being up the wall.

My partner being pregnant was a miracle. A miracle provided by a society that accepted my partner and me as family to each other, a legal system that allowed my name to go on my son's birth certificate as 'other parent', and the most overwhelmingly generous present from friends anyone could ever have.

In our antenatal class there were 12 sets of parents. Nearly all of us in our thirties, nearly all white, nearly all well-off. Six about-to-be-parents became pregnant 'the usual way', six sets of parents had required 'intervention'. I'm pretty sure the other five 'interventionist' couples thought we'd gone through some expensive and invasive medical procedure to combat our 'social infertility'.

We didn't tell them about The Masterbatorium.

Parenting confessions

BY THE SPINOFF PARENTS

When The Spinoff Parents put the call out for dirty little secrets and confessions about parenting, it was inundated by text, email and private message.

* I have a favourite child. I try not to, and I don't think my other kids would ever know. But I really like my first-born the most. He's the calmest and the quietest. I feel mean for thinking that, but we have such a special bond and my other kid is such a massive pain in the ass.

* I once spent an hour in public with poo on my forehead before someone told me.

* When my baby was born, it took me a while to bond with them because I thought they'd be the opposite gender. It was as if I had to mourn the loss of the other baby who never existed before I could fall in love with the one I actually had.

* I have fed everyone in our house, including myself, food off the floor. The same floor that one of us may have pissed on.

* I purposely suck up my daughter's Lego in the vacuum cleaner and I love it.

* I look at my baby and think: a face only a mother would love. I look at my husband and we both giggle and whisper to each other at the same time: 'So ugly!'

* I pay my daughter two dollars to bring me my pants on cold mornings so I can get changed under the blankets.

* My child once pushed over another child at the park, and when the child's mother came over, I said it wasn't my child. It was so satisfying. She said, 'What a little shit!' and I agreed, because he was being a little shit.

* I sometimes get fully dressed to take my daughter to preschool, and when I get home I get back into PJs for my home-office job.

* When my baby was born I was horrified by how ugly he was. He is much cuter now.

* Sometimes I pretend my children belong to someone else so I can be more patient with them.

* During a playdate, I caught my five-year-old and his friend playing with my vibrator — they were using it as a microphone. I grabbed it and hid it. I've never told anyone that.

* My daughter hits me all the time. She gave me a black eye once and I had to say I walked into a door. She's four and I'm scared she's a psychopath.

* My wife's parents said they'd take our kids for the night so we could go to a wedding. It was our first time childless in four years. We bought some weed to have a sneaky sesh before the wedding (our first in about six years). We got super baked, had sex on the couch, then accidentally fell asleep right after and missed the wedding. We slept from 4 p.m. until the morning. It was awesome. We told our friends we got the wedding date wrong.

* I miss my old life so much it hurts. I miss everything about it. I really miss being selfish. Not just being able to watch TV whenever I want but also being spontaneous. I miss fancy dinners. My children are such fuckwits in restaurants.

* On more than one occasion I have helped my son search the house for his chocolate that I ate.

* If the kids wet the bed at night and I can get away with it, I will just put a towel down and deal with it in the morning.

* I eat my husband's treats and blame the kids.

* I sometimes answer my children by whispering, 'Why don't you go and show Daddy that?'

* I tell my son the bath is closed at least once a week

because I can't be fucked. Same goes for parks and anything he wants to do that I don't really.

* I use bath time as an opportunity to sit in the corner and catch up on Twitter.

* Sometimes I organise playdates just to hang out with mums that I think are cool.

* I let my four-year-old rummage through her siblings' school lunches at the end of each day and eat whatever she can find, even if it's been on the floor. I call it developing independent foraging skills.

* I intentionally buy my son pyjamas that can pass as clothes in case I run out of time to dress him in the morning.

* I gave my kid chilli chocolate and told her that all chocolate tastes like that, so I'd never have to share my stash.

* I've let my kids wag school just because I didn't want to adult that day.

* I've told people that my kids have nits just so I don't have to go see them.

* I sometimes put my fourth child to bed in her clothes so I don't have to get her dressed in the morning. And by sometimes, I mean every night.

* I blocked the toilet at home and blamed it on my son.

* I do not live for my children. I love them and I love our family, even our family life, but I don't feel obsessed with them or anxious when I'm not with them. I don't feel guilty when I drop them off at daycare (once I knew they were happy and settled in and well taken care of). I enjoy the relationship they have with their grandparents and am happy for them to have them whenever they want to. I don't pine for them while they're with them, but I do love seeing them again when they get home.

How to successfully take a shit after giving birth

BY SEMIRA DAVIS

Semira Davis is a writer and mother of one. She likes to read picture books and sing freestyle nursery rhymes. Her work often speaks of bodily functions, and the stuff that comes out of them.

Ladies aren't supposed to talk about shit — but we do. We also do late-night Google searches in the hope of figuring out how to physically manage a thing that used to be quite natural.

See, this is what happens after you give birth. The simple act of taking a shit is no longer simple. There's a process.

Before I had my baby, I was warned about the first afterbirth shit — how it would feel like you were giving birth all over again. I felt the opposite. When I was pushing to deliver I was annoyed at the constant feeling that I was trying to shit, but with no shit happening (or at least if it did they were polite about it, and were not telling me about it).

I was told that, after delivery, taking a shit would feel like birth again. Not for me. They felt splendid! There's nothing as pleasant as giving a push and having only a turd pop out, instead of a human head.

However, I found taking a shit did now need to be approached with caution. I'd had an episiotomy, and the midwife suggested I put pressure on my sutures in those first few weeks of pooing. And so the process began . . .

I felt guilty for doing an unlatch-and-dash whenever the sudden urge to poo arrived — scrambling to get all my equipment together before shitting myself. Sometimes I'd forget something and have to call out to whoever was in the house to bring me what I needed.

The worst was constipation. I'd much rather shit myself than be a new mum with new-mum hormones keeping me fused to my baby yet hearing them cry because they're hungry while I'm sitting on the toilet with half a shit hanging out of my asshole that's too thick to break off even if I tried — because, actually, I have tried!

This is where kiwifruit and pressure help. Eat a bunch of kiwifruit to loosen up the bowels. For me, it felt like I had clay clogged up in me — stuck to the walls! The fruit helped loosen it up and move it down smoothly. But by that point it had already been in there a while — plus I'd been sitting down most of the day doing feeds — so everything was just piled up like a Blues Brothers car-crash. So I could find myself facing a shit which was possibly too big to fit out of me.

You know how rocks can be put into a glass of water to make the water overflow? That's what pressure on the perineum was like for me. If I pressed my knuckles in, the force inward pushed something outward. Even nine weeks after the birth — well after my sutures had dissolved — if I held pressure on my perineum I could do my shit in a matter of minutes. Then I could get back to the baby and not have to sit there feeling helpless with a shit dangling out of my arse.

It took some trial and error, but here is my recipe for taking a shit after giving birth.

Equipment needed:
3–6 kiwifruit, consumed during the day
1 x watering can or jug, filled with warm water (not hot!)
1 x clean sanitary/nursing pad, or a wad of toilet paper (toilet paper usually leaves wet bits stuck to your gooch, but you have the water to wash it away)

Step 1: Have you eaten some kiwifruit today? Feel like taking a shit? Good! Offload the baby to someone, or put them in a safe place so you can dash away to begin this adventure.

Step 2: Get your equipment. Make sure you have everything beforehand. I would take a new pad to change into afterwards, then use the cleanest part of the removed one for support. But if you'd rather not use the end of an old pad, perhaps use a clean nursing pad instead. I actually used my old nursing pads too, sometimes — waste not want not!

Step 3: Hold the pad on your perineum. Nestle it in there, all nice and cosy. Don't be afraid to apply pressure — the more the better, I found, so long as you're not aiming to punch through it.

Step 4: Push to poo like you would normally. As soon as you push, apply that pressure on the pad as much as you can. I used the knuckles of my fingers pressed against the pad. Keep the pressure in place until the very end of your shit. I know, it's much nicer to use that hand to scroll through articles on your phone about all the things you're now wanting answers to, but trust me — you're gonna want to hold on!

Now, be aware; you'll probably piss on your hand. But birth and its aftermath are no place to be scared of bodily fluids. If you pee while applying pressure, do not bother moving your hand away. Soap can fix that.

If you happen to know your bodily cues and know you are going to pee either before or after your poo, use the jug/watering can to pour water directly into your urine stream — that will take the sting out. With the pad and pressure in place you usually don't feel much sting anyway — then you can just wring out the pad and chuck it in the bin, then stare at the wall thinking back on the days when you didn't regularly urinate on yourself.

Step 5: Treat yourself to a nice rinse off. Pour all that lovely warm water down there. Get rid of all the sticky stuff you weren't prepared to still have coming out of you that's clinging to your pubes. Wash off the urine. Get rid of any leftovers, so that the only wiping you'll need to do is more of a pat dry. Because if you're like me and needed to have sutures put in, then they'll likely be dissolvable, and bits of cotton can appear on the toilet paper when you wipe. The first time I saw this I thought I had worms. That was a fun day.

Step 6: Go get that beautiful baby, and triumphantly praise yourself for having just successfully taken a shit!

Helpful hint: Avoid in-water toilet cleaners. I share a house and one was put in straight after my delivery, so the water was bright blue. I was not keen on getting that up in a delicate flesh wound. An extra step was to scrunch up some toilet paper and throw it in the bowl beforehand, to dull the splash-back.

Same DNA, same brain, same sleep patterns — right? What being a twin mum has taught me about child sleep

BY ANGELA CUMING

Angela Cuming is a print and radio journalist. She has three boys under three and hasn't slept in five years.

Identical twins, they say, are a miracle of nature. No one knows exactly how or why they are created, all we know is that from the day of their birth they share a beautiful bond and are completely in sync with each other.

As the mother of identical twin baby boys, please excuse me while I use the last of my energy reserves to die laughing.

My identical twins, who are 16 months old, are nothing,

nothing alike, especially when it comes to one critical area: sleep.

Henry, our little angel from birth, slept through the night from when he was two months old. But Terrible Tommy has woken me up two, three, four times a night for I would say, oh, 16 months or so.

Right from the get-go Tommy was trouble. Both twins spent 12 nights in NICU and while Henry was a textbook patient, Tommy would give the poor nurses grief. He would buck and wriggle in his little incubator so much he'd set off alarms. He'd rip the wires monitoring his heartbeat off his chest — twice they thought he had stopped breathing — and pulled a drip from his ankle.

'He will be fine once you get him home, give him a couple of weeks,' the nurses said, as they all but threw him into our waiting car.

The six-week milestone came and went, then the three-month mark, and Tommy would still wake every two hours at night, screaming and snuffling and vomiting.

And all the while his twin brother slept.

I was doing nothing different with either of them. A feeding diary shows both were fed almost exactly the same amount each day, at the same time. As they grew and I stopped waking them at night for feeds, Henry would sleep on through while Tommy would still wake.

And it would kill me, it really would, watching one baby sleeping peacefully while the other one wailed and kicked their legs. Being identical means they have exactly the same DNA. The egg was fertilised and, for whatever reason, split into two. They are in effect the **EXACT SAME BABY WITH THE SAME BRAIN**. Why on God's earth did one brain want to sleep and the other want to go clubbing all night, every night?

I tried a dummy, he would spit it out. I tried patting his bum and shushing him back to sleep — he'd look at me the way you would a Trump supporter when they tell you the president cares about the working class.

I tried barging into the spare room where my husband was sleeping at 2 a.m. (we took turns on night duty), plopping Tommy on the bed and saying 'Here, have a baby.' That worked, but only for that night.

Tommy then developed the charming habit of banging his head against the cot mattress to 'self-soothe' himself back to sleep. And making a horrible 'mwa mwa mwa' noise while he did it.

By the six-month mark I was shattered, and began to visit Dante's tenth circle of hell — googling 'how to get your baby to sleep through the night'.

There was controlled crying — not so good when he shares a room with another baby. And it didn't work. I guarantee you that baby would cry until Hypercolor t-shirts were back in fashion rather than roll over and drift off to sleep.

'He's too cold!' another expert told me. So I followed their advice and used a sleeping bag and the recommended 15 (I know!) layers of light blankets. He just got tangled like hair around a scrunchie and, I suspect, overheated.

I stuffed him full of food before bedtime, he got a tummy upset. I fed him lots and lots of milk, he spewed.

I read all the books about twins. I tried to put them on the same routine, but rather suspect the authors of that advice have never actually cared for one baby, let alone two at a time. All that happens is you have not one but two screaming, hungry babies on your hands and neither gets fed properly so neither sleeps properly.

I'd try sleeping with Tommy on the couch. He'd think it was party time and would crawl around the floor, bashing toy cars together. We co-slept and he wriggled around so much he fell off the bed. I used mobiles, white noise, a metronome, took all the toys out of his cot, put them all back in, changed the mattress, the bedding, read to him, sang to him, and still that child would not sleep through the night.

I put a *Teletubbies* toy in his cot that would light up and play 'Twinkle Twinkle Little Star' as a means to soothe him to sleep. He would activate that horrible little toy and shine it into his brother's cot to wake him so he would have someone to talk to.

Laa-Laa has now gone on holidays.

Tommy wasn't much better during the day, either. Henry would giggle and coo and stare out a window at the clouds for hours at a time. Often he would curl up on the floor and nap like a cat during the day. Once I forgot he was there and went to bed myself, only realising hours later that he was still on a rug in the corner of the living room.

Tommy once crawled up to me with a giant earthworm stuck on the back of his head.

And now, here we are at the 16-month mark and Tommy still head-bangs, and still wakes two or three times a night.

So what can parents take from this? If sleep is all about your parenting — what's the deal with my twins? Surely the consolation for you (given I'm up all night, there has to be a bright side) is that this clearly shows all kids are different. Some are sleepers and some are *not sleepers*. It's really that simple. There can be no other explanation.

I've sat on that nursery floor at 3 a.m. sobbing into my hands, slammed doors at 4 a.m. and pleaded with him at 5 a.m.: 'If you go to sleep now, I promise you I will buy you a car when you turn sixteen, we can work this out.' I've tried to work it out.

I still treat each baby the same. They eat the same food, drink the same amount of milk, are awake during the day for the same amount of time, both crawl the same and use their walkers the same and have a bath together and get the same amount of love and cuddles and attention and OH MY GOD WHY WON'T YOU SLEEP LIKE YOUR BROTHER???!!!

And then I watch them playing together outside, Henry picking daisies from the lawn and Tommy eating dirt and an apple core left inside a possum trap, and I realise they are just that, brothers. Not the same person, not the same brain. Two perfect little humans who, although identical twins, have their own personalities and traits and ways of sleeping.

And I remember those seven long, long months I carried those two babies, who shared only one placenta and who had only a small shot at making it all the way. I remember the twice-weekly scans to find out whether Tommy was still with us, the agonising moment he was taken from my arms and rushed to neo-natal intensive care and I think, you know what, my son? You have all the time in the world to sleep.

Staring at the night sky: Reaching a diagnosis and saving our daughter

BY JESSIE MOSS

Jessie Moss is a primary-school teacher, musician, writer, keen runner and Te Reo Māori enthusiast who lives in Newtown, Wellington, with her partner and their two daughters.

The day had arrived and we were eager to get on with it. As four adults sat awkwardly around a child-size table for sick and healing kids, and our toddler bustled and boomed, our eldest daughter sucked her thumb. She cocked her head to the side, sitting in a rare quietness that told us she was listening intently.

The surgeon explained the procedure again, in plain language that even Mataamua could mostly understand. We asked a few questions, as did she.

'Will the knife be a kids' knife?' she asked. 'And will it cut softly?'

'Yes, of course, it will cut very carefully,' replied the paediatric surgeon.

We all understood there is never any point in frightening an already anxious child.

At 7.30 a.m., during the pre-surgery formalities, the surgeon also told us something new. The removal of Mataamua's benign tumours was never optional, as we had assumed. Inevitably, the surgeon said, they would turn malignant.

The gravity of the situation sank in.

He understood — there was no point in stressing already worried parents. A world expert, he had done this all before.

So, at the eleventh hour, we realised that all of our research, reading, persistence and insistence had in fact saved our daughter's life.

Left undiagnosed, people with these tumours don't become grandparents, or even parents. But genetics has only just got to this point, predicting what bodies are likely to do in time.

They were removed with expertise, precision, care. Her recovery was swift and uncomplicated. We left hospital on time, and carried on with our Christmas and summer as planned. After several weeks, Mataamua could swim again, and in several weeks to come, she will ride a horse once more.

Mataamua is almost seven and she is missing a bunch of genes.

A section of one of her chromosomes fell out completely during the fertilisation process. It is not inherited and it was entirely unpredictable. The effects on her development are global. In her body, her mind, her growth and socialisation.

But you need a sharp eye to spot her differences. Some teachers and health professionals can see them, but we've even had to explain the complexities of her syndrome to close friends who have known her all her life. It is an invisible syndrome of sorts and this makes raising and supporting her all the more challenging.

The months preceding her surgery whooshed by in a blur of appointments. These months made up for the years of confusion, the sluggish pace at which we were passed from specialist to specialist, from wait-list to wait-list.

No one ever seemed to know what was going on. Guesses and suggestions were thrown around month upon month. Even in my mind, what she 'had' would change as often as the direction of wind in this blustery town. One thing, however, remained constant: well-meaning people assuring us that it didn't matter what she 'had' but how we dealt with it.

I agreed and I understood the intent.

We are to love our children unconditionally and we must meet their needs, no matter who or what they are. However, how are we to know what a child's needs are when we don't know the finer details, or how they may change as they grow? Or when a child seems more and more out of step with their peers with each passing year?

A small birth-weight and slowness to latch weren't unusual and were swiftly attended to when our baby was born. Digestive issues with solids are not unheard of. Slight delays in crawling, walking and talking were all still on the charts, if not at the bottom end. Plenty of toddlers get obsessed with narrow fields of play. Lots of young children are overly friendly, and many more still have huge, regular tantrums. Some kids take a really long time to become adept at riding a scooter or climbing up ladders.

All these things and more concerned us. For any child, their universe expands as they grow. More and more lights are switched on and many connections are made. For Mataamua, it was as if a grey fog was growing at the same rate as her universe, which was either swallowing her stars, or obscuring them from our view. Younger friends met milestones before she did.

We second-guessed ourselves and friends and doctors reassured us. But the older she got, the more the grey expanse grew.

This all sounds horribly negative and bleak. It's not. Mataamua is a beautiful, empathetic and sharp girl. She is an avid listener of music and books. She loves the outdoors and would also watch TV all day if she could (not unlike many kids). But for us to meet her differing needs, and to support her best, we needed to look closely at her. We needed to focus on the differences and we needed to take our concerns to specialists.

We knew there was an alternative picture emerging. And it was a different night sky. An endlessly beautiful but puzzling night sky.

When she was three, an early childhood teacher took me aside and described what she saw. Defensive at first, it took me a moment to stop and listen. Kids behave differently with other adults. Their chemistry is changed and their environment is altered. Mataamua's teacher had an insight that we did not. We added her observations to the growing pile of letters detailing various physiological issues.

By the time she started school, there was no doubt that something was amiss.

Still, we were told not to worry and that all kids lag in one area or another. We were told that some kids tire more easily. That some kids are prone to sensory overload. It didn't matter what she had, but how we parented her.

Speech and language therapists, dietitians, paediatricians, our GP, occupational therapists, parenting courses, respite care. You name it.

And then — a geneticist.

One test revealed all.

It pointed us and several doctors to new areas to assess that wouldn't have been explored otherwise. This included the discovery of tumours, and it explained so much about our girl.

We did all of this as university-educated parents. I am a teacher — often for children with additional learning needs. We come from a large and supportive family consisting of counsellors, social workers, social activists and artists. We are health literate — and it was still difficult.

It wasn't that people were resisting our pursuit for answers, but that each person was looking at the night sky from their own particular place in the world. We, however, viewed her sky from the same perspective.

I never would have guessed a rare syndrome, and certainly wouldn't have been looking for tumours.

Diagnosis does matter, if there is one to be found. With it comes resources. Knowledge. New support networks.

Friends often describe her spark, her immediate radiant warmth. I can't imagine a more bleak night sky without my shining Mataamua. She — and we — all need as many bright stars as we can get.

Six key benefits of extreme sleep deprivation inflicted by a tiny human or tiny humans

BY MICHELLE COURSEY

Michelle Coursey is a full-time mum to her five-month-old daughter, and a some-time writer, editor and social media manager.

So, you're about to become a parent, and all people seem to say to you these days is 'Get that sleep while you still can' and 'Forget about ever sleeping in again for the next 43 years'. And it's got you terrified.

Sleep — that magical, wondrous healing elixir — is about to be snatched away by a pair of tiny, adorable hands. Don't freak out though. What no one has told you are the little known benefits of never sleeping for more than three hours at a time, and existing on the sweet dreamy memory fumes of that one night you slept from 10 p.m. to 4 a.m. (then woke up in a sweaty panic of nightmarish proportions to wonder what the hell had happened to your baby).

SLEEP DEPRIVATION CAN RESULT IN SOME SERIOUS *BENJAMIN BUTTON*-ING

Maybe it's the fact that I have been forced to constantly wear jeans and a loose singlet (for access to the all-important boobs at any time), or that most mornings I have to choose between getting to pee on my own or putting mascara on (solo pee wins every time, FYI), but the end result is that I've been ID'ed more in the past six months than any other time in the past five years. Sure, I have bags under my eyes that are darker than the black soul of Scarface Claw, and my hair looks like some kind of performance-art experiment, but I look like I could be under 25 according to the 19-year-old Pak'nSave checkout girl, so fuck yeah. #winning

YOU WILL BE ABLE TO WITHSTAND ANY KIND OF INTERROGATION FROM EVIL FORCES

Should you find yourself in the evil lair of an international villain who is seeking to discover all of New Zealand's deepest, darkest secrets (no one really likes L&P; *The Lord of the Rings* movies were definitely too long; our summer is less beach weather, more monsoon season), do not sweat it. Because once you have gone 10 rounds with a screaming baby from 11 p.m. to 2 a.m., and can still get up in the morning and figure out how to get the baby carrier with one bazillion straps correctly tied and configured, forget breaking down under the bright lights of a torture chamber and spilling everything. You'll outlast anyone.

CASH ME AT 3.37 A.M.

Not sure why every meme you see says 'Cash me ousside' or features Chris Warner's head exploding over someone's dick pic? You will never have to wonder again because you have So. Much. Time. to read the internet in the middle of the night. Especially when your delightful little cherub wakes up to practice those really essential rolling skills in the middle of the night for an hour and a half, and you're dying inside with the thirst of a thousand suns for sleep, but they cry every time you close your eyes. Just give up and read the internet. All of it. How bow dah, you tiny insane human Energizer bunny.

CHECK OUT THAT SUNRISE, INSTA-BITCHES

OK, so you are definitely not in a state to be 'gramming your kale smoothie resting on your muscular, Lycra-clad tights at an early morning park workout session. Or a slightly off-centre Valencia-filter snap of you and your bestie chugging espresso martinis at the hottest nightclub (#nightofmylife #paaaaarty). However, when you stumble out of the front gate at 4.45 a.m. — in your pyjama pants and jandals, with a small pudgy dictator strapped to your front — prepared to walk to Cape Reinga and back if it will just make her sleep another hour, you will get some amazing shots of the sunrise/moody suburban streets thick with fog/old men walking their dogs in short shorts to make all your followers jealous of the thrilling life you lead. #nofilter

THIS IS HOW WE LIVE NOW. ADAPT OR DIE.

No one likes boring chores like tidying the house, preparing nutritious meals, wearing clean clothes or paying bills in a timely manner, right? Well, my friends, sleep deprivation takes care of all that for you, with the ultimate excuse to never do any of it again.

Oh, you think I should have vacuumed the floor which is covered in three-day old raisins and dead flies? I had exactly 95 minutes of sleep last night and even that was with tiny feet kicking me in the thigh so hard I'm bruised. Walk around the corpses. You wanted dinner ready before 10 p.m.? I lost count of the number of times I got up to 'resettle' and ended up sleeping in a small pool of milky vomit. Get out the takeaway brochures, fool.

NAPS ARE NOW COMPULSORY

Yes, you read that right. It's now actually compulsory to snuggle on into the duvet and nap to your heart's content (actually, you can nap as long as your baby allows you to before their eyes open and they start screeching like a banshee, which is probably about 15 minutes after you finally manage to get to sleep). But seriously, people tell you to nap all the time, and if you open the door at 3.30 p.m. with bedhead and your daggy trackies on, you may even be praised for your sensible approach to life. And to be honest, when you eventually see that peaceful little face finally succumb to the sleep gods, and you get to close your eyes, everything suddenly feels pretty great. Heavenly, even. Screw the eye bags and the inability to multiply any number higher than three. Sleep is for the weak anyway, right?

A recording was made of a mother one morning, beginning at 5 a.m.

BY EMILY WRITES

Shhh . . . shh . . . Mama's here. Turituri! It's still night-time. Night-time. Bottle? Shhh! Don't wake your brother.

No, go back to sleep honey, your brother just wants a bottle. No, it's still night-time. No, you can't watch Peppa. It's night time. Turituri.

OK, fine. No yelling. Please no whining. Inside voices. Inside voices, please.

Is that the way you talk to Mama, please? Is that your kind voice?

Oh, thank you for the cuddle. Ātaahua!
What would you like for breakfast?
Hello? Can anyone hear me?
Is Mama talking to herself? What do you want for breakfast?
Don't hit your brother, please.
Inside voices.

Be gentle. Gentle hands. Is that how we treat each other? We don't bite. Stop yelling, please.

I SAID STOP YELLING. OK? WE ARE KIND IN THIS HOUSE!

OK, pancakes! Mīharo! Careful, please. Don't spill — OK, don't worry, Mama will clean it up. Get your hands out of it, please. Ināianei tonu. HANDS OUT! I SAID HANDS OUT! WHAT DID I SAY? Thank you, my darling heart.

OK, clothes on please. Can we please wear normal clothes? Underwear goes on the inside. You don't have to wear shorts over pants. OK, fine. Leave your brother alone. You worry about you, please, I'll worry about him. I'm his mum, not you. You're his brother.

Teeth. Teeth. Teeth. If you don't brush them properly they will all fall out and nobody will want to marry you. No, you don't have to get married. No, it was a joke. No, you can't marry me — I'm already married. You can't marry your brother. OK, fine, calm down, you can marry him.

Get that out of your brother's face. Don't lick your brother. Stop it. Stop now. Whakarongo mai.

Shoes please.
E noho.
Shoes.
E noho.
Shoes.
Shoes.
E noho.
I'm not saying it again.
Don't make me say it again.
Shoes.
Shoes please.
I am not saying it again.
SHOES.
I SAID PUT YOUR SHOES ON RIGHT NOW.
SHOES! FOR THE LOVE OF GOD PUT YOUR SHOES ON!
No yelling please. I SAID NO YELLING! WE ARE GOING TO HAVE A

GOOD DAY IF YOU JUST PUT YOUR SHOES ON.

Thank you, my darling.

I don't understand when you use that voice. No whingeing please, just tell me. Use your words. Words please. Slower and I will be able to understand. Use your words. Use your words.

Did you take your shoes off? Put them back on!

Don't make me count to three.

I'm going to count to three.

One.

I'm going to count to three.

Two.

Don't make me get to three.

One. Two.

Whakarongo mai!

PUT YOUR SHOES ON OR I WILL GET TO THREE.

Do you need to go wharepaku?

Thank you my angel heart. Mama loves you.

OK, we are going to be late. Jump in the car. Huri mai. OK, all buckled in? What? You need to go toilet now? Why didn't you go before? OK, fine, yes, good, thank you for telling me. OK, come on. Ka pai.

SHOES.

Hands out of your pants please.

Because I said so.

PUT YOUR SHOES — yes, wipe please. You can wipe yourself, you don't need me to do it.

Horoia ō ringaringa. Now. Wash. Hands.

OK, back in the car. Tino pai!

STOP SHOUTING!

Out of the car please. Careful. Hold hands. Hold hands. Don't run. There's cars. PLEASE LISTEN *whispers* I will give you a Kinder Surprise if you walk nicely.

Kindy is fun! You will have a great day. Ka kite. Ka kite. Mama has to go. Ka kite. Ka kite. Bye my love. No, really, I have to go. I have to go. I have to. Ka kite. Ka kite. See you soon! I love you. Mama loves you. Moon and stars. Yes, I do. Be good. Love you. Ka kite. I have to go. I have to. Ka kite.

Stay-at-home dadding — the reality

BY ADAM MAMO

Full-time dad and sometime freelance writer, Adam Mamo writes about parenting and related madness from Auckland.

Many months ago, I switched dad codes from the full-time employed variety to the stay-at-home type, with a toddler and a baby. The swap not only brought significant challenges but also regular questions from other dads. 'What's it like *really*?' And 'How hard is it . . . honestly?'

There seemed to be a suspicion from dark corners of the dad world about the true difficulty of full-time parenting. Far-fetched ideas that it's all just some unified scam by mums to stay out of the workforce, sip coffee at cafés and enjoy the delights of daytime television.

The first time I was asked how hard it is, I'd been on the job just a few weeks and replied, 'Those mum blogs make you think it's tougher than deep sea fishing off the Alaskan coast, but it's not actually that hard.'

I'd soon realise that response was like jogging one kilometre before decreeing that marathon running is easy. Now, I've seen some shit. And experienced moments when I'd gladly trade my position for the decks of a breezy fishing vessel.

Before I scuttle the bright-eyed optimism of dads seeking the truth, it's important to start with the positives. Being a stay-at-home dad is one of the most courageous and hardcore things a modern man can do. Lasting bonds are built with your kids and sacrifices made are rewarded through self-growth and the discovery of new skills and strengths.

Now it's time to harpoon any misconceptions that stay-at-home dadding is 'living the dream'.

FORGET ABOUT RECOGNITION

There's no industry award for Best New Stay-at-Home Dad and there's certainly no promotion or pay rise. If you're accustomed to regular butt-pats and kudos, it'll be a shock to your reinforcement-requiring system. From your partner, recognition will flow early but can quickly morph into expectation. Relentless self-motivation and a stoic attitude are key attributes for successful long-term stay-at-home dadding.

Additionally, coming home each evening to be received like a niche-sport world champ parading down Queen Street is over. You're no longer the cool parent, the carefree, fun one who turns a blind eye to jumping on the sofa and risks nappy-bag-free trips out. Bridle up, mate, for the shift from show pony to workhorse.

YOU'LL NEVER BE ALONE BUT YOU'LL FEEL ALONE

It's difficult to avoid feeling isolated. Your world shrink-wraps around you and it becomes clear you're a minority. The search for like-minded dads to chill with during the week can be arduous. 'Parents groups' are mostly just mummy groups that claim to be inclusive but don't need your type in their ranks.

Why not? A functioning mums' group is complex and requires certain roles to be filled. There's the ex-middle-management mum, who complains about always organising but refuses help, the struggling-to-cope mum with the naughty kid and, of course, the anti-vax mum that's a constant topic of private online chats outside the group. What a mums' group doesn't need is some dad contaminating this delicate ecosystem.

The best bet for work-hours company is more informal; locate other day-walker dads in your area, meet weekly at a park, split a six-pack and watch your kids wrestle. Talk sport and cars, exaggerate about how badass you were before becoming a dad, complain a lot, then when everyone starts crying — go home.

Sorted.

IT'S MORE PHYSICAL THAN YOU'D THINK

Surprisingly so. Picking up a 15kg toddler ain't nothing, right? Not the first time, but by the hundredth time that day, it is a thing. Combined with other dad-related physical trials like car-seat installation, nappy-bin clearing and teeth-brushing restraint — it's a workout. While there isn't one single action that will put massive strain on you, the combination of all of them, with tiredness thrown in, certainly will.

Mums know this, and many do yoga for reasons beyond postpartum recovery — it assists with the twisting and strength required for bossing young kids all day. Unfortunately, the world isn't ready to see you spray-foamed into yoga pants, downward dogging. Until times change, wear good trainers and bend at the knees when lifting.

YOU'LL HEAR IGNORANT CRAP ON THE DAILY

Is there still some stigma around being a stay-at-home dad? Absolutely. The concept of a grown-ass man staying home and raising kids still doesn't compute in certain areas of our society.

Naturally, you'll cop cheap shots from mates. 'So when does the man of the house get home?', and many phrases that include the word 'mangina'. Clever stuff for sure. The heavier hits may come from family; perhaps your dad introduces you to friends by saying you're 'in between jobs'. Random old ladies will jump to conclusions: 'Have you taken the day off to give Mum a break?' And then there's shadowing assumptions: 'Maybe he lost his job', 'Is he depressed?', 'Only a depressed guy would wear a grey cardigan.'

The most bullshit thing I've heard (anecdotally) said to a stay-at-home dad is, 'Why are you doing the job of a 14-year-old girl?' Without insulting the abilities of 14-year-old girls, that's going to make any dad feel face-punchy.

Being a stay-at-home dad in New Zealand still challenges social expectations. While that remains the case, the old-fashioned, the unfiltered and the macho dinosaurs are still going to blurt out ignorant crap. Respond with anything from a polite smile to an accidental head-butt, or just make like a three-year-old and use your words.

YOU WON'T BE SCRATCHING YOUR NUTS WATCHING TEST CRICKET

The real heartbreaker for prospective stay-at-home dads is the reality of how much time you'll have to yourself on weekdays. Consider how much time you think you'll have doing your own thing, halve that, and then halve it again for two kids, and again for a third. That's about how much time you'll have — on your best day.

The problem here is that the language surrounding the concept is a trap: 'Are you finishing work to look after the kids?' or 'It must be so nice not to work.' In reality, it's usually a full day's work and then some. Dreams of lowering golf handicaps or starting a profitable online business while 'being off work' are going to be difficult to execute.

It's also tough for new full-time dads to accept that any day where 'all they do' is parent the kids has been a successful day and an achievement in itself.

YOU'RE NOT GOING TO BE THE GREATEST DAD IN THE ENTIRE UNIVERSE

'If being a dad was all I had to do, I'd be the best dad ever!' That's a sweet notion, rookie, and full credit for the misguided ambition. But it's a survival situation, not an opportunity to chase empty accolades.

Also, teaching baby sign language or mastering your little girl's French braid isn't as easy as you may think. A vital part of full-time parenting is identifying the limitations of all parties involved, especially your own, and having clear processes and routines in place. If you aim for dadding that's competent and confident then one day you may just unwrap a tacky 'World's Greatest Dad' coffee mug. Claim it then.

Sadly, what grinds down many fresh stay-at-home dads isn't the strains of the job, but the external perception of it, the feelings of isolation and even the self-inflicted career damage. However, people will say dumb things regardless of what you do, and total career duration greatly exceeds the short window when your children are in their earliest stages of development.

Most dads are faced with financial and other reasons why being a stay-at-home dad isn't viable. If it is possible, and entered into with open eyes and a steely resolve, it's a massively rewarding way to spend a few months or a few years. It's the type of testing journey that isn't easy to find within monotonous modern lifestyles.

By going full-time dad you'll not only add a rich experience to your own life — your advocating of it will help reinforce what other stay-at-home dads achieved before you, and make it easier for other fathers that follow.

Defending being defensive about co-sleeping

BY EMILY WRITES

The other day I said to my husband 'I should really try to get the baby to sleep on his own tonight.' My husband smiled and gave me a hug. He knew that what I really meant was 'Tell me it's OK our baby is still in bed with us at night.'

There are lots of reasons why we co-sleep most nights. I went through a stage where I hid the fact that we were co-sleeping. I thought the measure of a mum who had her shit together was how well her children slept. I have never been a particularly confident mother, but as my children have grown I've started to see how our choices have worked really well for us as a family. This has helped me be a bit kinder to myself, to have more faith in my abilities.

Co-sleeping feels like one of those *half choice half obligation* things for us. If our child didn't want to co-sleep, we wouldn't co-sleep. So it's not entirely a choice, but it is a choice in that we are now comfortable with it as *the thing we do*.

Recently, my husband said to a sort-of-friend: 'Oh yeah, both of our kids are in our beds — usually I have one and Emily has the other'. I was shocked. 'Don't tell people!' I hissed. He was perplexed. 'It's nothing to be ashamed of. What's the big deal?'

This approach made me stop and think about my defences for co-sleeping, and what impact being secretive has on the judgement orgy around sleep. Then it made me consider that maybe I need to just let go of being defensive altogether.

Yet the next day, as I was waiting for my coffee, I heard a woman in the coffee shop lecturing her poor (maybe?) daughter-in-law on 'tough love' and how her child will never sleep on their own.

I was again, immediately defensive. I wanted to turn to her and say:

Yes, they have their own room. And yes, they have their own beds. But we trial and change approaches to see what works. It's almost like we are people who don't have all the answers and in fact don't believe that parenting is a game that you win or lose. It's almost like every child and every parent is different and we are working out what's best for us all.

Yes, we have tried putting them in their own room and saying 'stay in there'. Are we soft? Sure. But what's the downside to being soft? Surely in this world we live in we need more gentle parenting that is focused on the needs of the whole family? Being hard isn't what we are about. We don't want to be tough and we just don't believe that the downfall of humanity is due to our parenting decisions. Letting a child who had a nightmare (or wet the bed or just feels sick or can't sleep) into your bed is a little act of kindness that we, their parents — those who know them best — are happy to do. It's not for everyone, and it doesn't always work for us. But of the list of choices of what to do, we are most happy with the *cuddles for everything* approach.

We're not lazy but in all honesty — who cares if we are? Why is The Path Of Least Resistance Parenting so frowned upon?

Parenting isn't meant to be an ordeal. Why not make it easier?

No, you don't have to co-sleep. Honestly, it's not possible to put into words how little I care about how other parents parent at night. Lack of sleep is a killer. You need to do what's right for you. So you don't want kids in your bed? Fine with me. It's not my bed. I'd ask for the same courtesy though.

Yes, I have a happy marriage and yes, my husband is OK with our child sleeping with us. He's also happy to sleep in the bunk sometimes, or the spare room, just like I do. And you know what BERYL we actually have a really happy marriage because I get to watch him willingly choose to do what works for our family as a whole on a nightly (and daily) basis. It teaches me to compromise too. We make decisions together because we are both parents and we respect each other.

And yes, we have sex. I was once asked this when I was visibly very pregnant. It was not an immaculate conception.

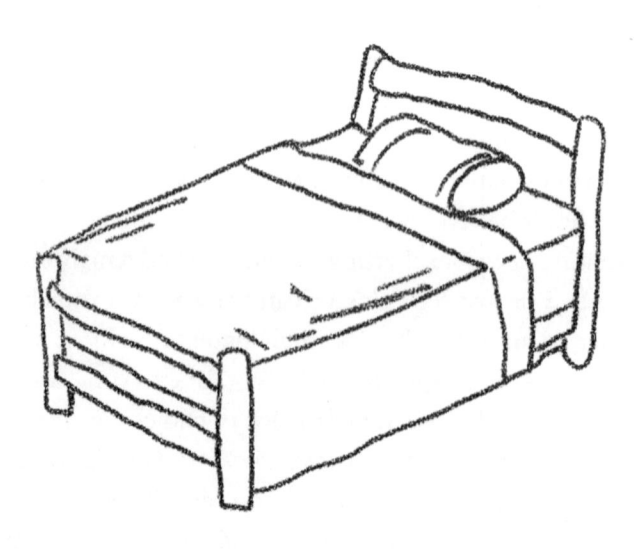

This might sound shocking, but there are other places to have sex that aren't a bed. I'm sorry you're so limited in imagination. But also, is it weird that you want to know? I guess I'd be fixated if the only time I did the deed was with the lights out in the marital bed.

And no our children aren't spoilt or out of control — we are a family that considers each other and tries to do what's best. For us. Only. Not you, not your family, just us. And for us, this works with our way of being a family and it works for the kids and it might be a hassle some nights but ultimately this is a *it'll be fine in the end/you're only little once* kind of approach.

No they won't be sleeping with us when they're 18 but I've never understood how the same people who say that also say that their children don't speak to them anymore and cherish every second of every minute of every hour of the day because soon you'll be alone, so alone. So alone that you fashion a dog out of pantyhose and newspaper and drag it around your living room saying 'Come Pepper! Mama is here!'

Yes, you're right — co-sleeping can really suck sometimes. Some days I do want to bitch about having a kid in my bed. But that doesn't mean I'm miserable about it or that things will be different tonight or that I'm doing the *wrong* thing. It just means I had a bad night. And being able to complain about it isn't an invitation for unsolicited advice. It's not a time to say: 'I've never had the kids in my bed and I never would I don't know how you do it just put them in their own bed don't you think it's time for them to sleep on their own.' If you do that, people (me) will think you suck.

Do I think it's time for a child to sleep on their own? Which child? What age? Here are some of the reasons why my children have returned to my bed for short periods:

* going back to work and they missed me

* growth spurt and they needed more milk

* family member died and they were scared of death

* threw up in bed then became concerned the bed was the reason why they spewed

* dog died and they were scared of zombie dogs

* 'I miss you'

* weekend away made them think I had disappeared forever

* afraid of giant ninja turtle but did not want to move giant ninja turtle out of their bed

* got confused on the way back from the bathroom

* every sleep regression on the planet

* brother was in bed so felt it was unfair they had to sleep alone

* started school and was feeling scared

Frankly, some of these are crap reasons to wake your parents up at night. But some of these are things I want my kids to wake me up to talk about. And some of these things are hard to discuss at 3 a.m. when you just want to go the fuck to sleep.

So ultimately I'm OK with saying — come on in.

I sleep better with my husband in bed, and sometimes I even sleep better with one of the kids in bed. I have times when I wake up and reach over for comfort. It makes sense that my kids look for the same. And while they're little, I'm happy to be able to answer that call.

I've heard it all and I don't need any advice anymore. I won't even humour people. Because I'm at the acceptance phase and it's kind of radical. We just aren't as bothered by a kid or kids in our bed (as long as it's *our* kid or kids) as other people seem to be bothered by a kid or kids in our bed.

Is this what it feels like to be comfortable in your parenting? Is this growing up?

Maybe it's just time; it just feels normal for us now. It feels like way less of a big deal than it did two years ago.

We have a solution so we don't need a solution. This isn't a problem for us, and if it's a problem for others . . . that isn't our problem.

Things might change tomorrow, next month, next year. But for now I'm happy accepting that I'm one of those people who likes to be close to the ones they love at night. And my kids are the same.

During the night, when my baby reaches for me, I think, this is just where I want you to be. And if that's weird, well, I'm weird. Because baby, you're perfect. And one more snuggle is just what we all need.

Fearless at five

BY NADINE ANNE HURA

Nadine Anne Hura (Ngāti Hine, Ngāpuhi) writes policy by day and essays by night. Her writing explores themes of identity, biculturalism, politics and parenting.

We came across the piano in the middle of a crowded airport terminal. We heard it before we saw it — incongruously beautiful notes sailing above the chaos of boarding calls and the urgent clack of wheels on tiles. A sign above the piano invited travellers to 'stop and play what makes you fly'.

As we passed, I felt Bobbie stop beside me. She grabbed my arm and pulled me back. 'Mummy!' she whispered. 'Can I play?'

I looked from the piano to her, and back to the piano. It was a baby grand, sleek in black with its great heart exposed for all to see. It was more like a rock than a piano. People flowed around it like rushing water. A young man with short cropped hair was playing something complicated and classical. Beethoven, Tchaikovsky — how would I know?

He finished playing, bowed low, then picked up his backpack and took off towards his gate.

With the stool vacated, Bobbie made a dash for it. I managed to stop her just in time, steering her towards a bookshop with buckets of trinkets and flags waving in the doorway.

She looked up at me, all polka-dot scarf and stripy top and bowler hat. 'Why won't you let me play?'

I sighed. She was five years old and ready for anything. The embroidered orange satchel she wore across her chest made it look like she was permanently strapped into a seatbelt. She hadn't worked out that there was a certain order to things. That there were times to put yourself forward, and times to hold yourself back.

By now there was another recital in full swing, a young woman this time. Her fingers fluttered so lightly over the keys it was like they were an extension of her own hands.

How to tell my girl in stripes and dots that 'Old MacDonald' couldn't follow Mozart, or whoever the hell it was . . .

But she insisted. 'I can play,' she said firmly. 'I am allowed.'

I lingered on those words. *I am allowed.* How unfazed she was by any doubt about her ability to contribute to this spontaneous outpouring of musical talent. A flicker of recognition passed through me. I had been like that too, once upon a time. I too had been unaware of any limits or ceilings or boundaries. My dream was to be a famous runner, like my hero John Walker. How many times had I replayed the video of him winning that 1500 m Olympic gold medal? As a 10-year-old, I saved up all my money and bought a pair of Arthur Lydiard running shoes. I can't remember growing out of the shoes, but I remember the feeling of self-doubt that took root soon after. I remember it, because I live with it still.

Then it dawned on me: by not letting my daughter play the piano because I was scared she'd embarrass herself, I was stripping her of the self-confidence she was born with. Who was I to do that? If she wasn't embarrassed, why should *I* be? Let her embrace her self-confidence for as long as she can. Nurture it so it flourishes.

'All right,' I said. 'You can play.'

She clenched her fists in victory and shouted 'Yuss!' so loudly that her brothers groaned and pretended they didn't know her. She rushed to stand behind the girl at the piano, as if forming a queue.

When at last the young woman finished and gave up the stool, Bobbie rubbed her hands together as if to prepare, and sat down. She put her shoulders back, took a deep breath and placed her fingers upon the keys.

As I listened to her play, not a single note out of time, I thought of parents who have to push their children out of their comfort zone to even do the slightest thing that might draw attention to themselves. I thought of her own brothers, wishing to disappear into the walls just by virtue of being related to her at this very moment. I thought of myself, still wrestling with the voice that says: you are not allowed.

And here was my daughter (my daughter!) playing 'Old MacDonald' in the middle of an enormous international airport with hundreds of people gazing upon her as they walked by. She played that baby grand like it was her gift to the world. Counting beats in her head, teeth biting bottom lip, every note seemed to say: 'I am allowed.'

When she finished, the applause was even louder and more generous than it had been for any one of the accomplished pianists before her. Apparently, Old MacDonald can follow any old song.

Bobbie stood up, bowed low, then skipped back to my side.

'Did I do well?' she asked, looking up at me with stripy spots.

'You were fearless,' I said.

When you're tired enough: On the hell of having a child who just won't sleep

BY EMILY WRITES

At night my home is a horror film.

Screams reverberate off the ceilings. There is no peace.

My son came into the world screaming and every night since he has screamed as if he is being forced into the world all over again.

During the day he is a mostly happy little boy whose hobbies include putting things on top of things, collecting shoes, giggling, cat chasing and eating grapes.

But he will not sleep. Especially at night.

And every time he does fall asleep he wakes terrified. He screams for us, his little heart racing, his face washed with tears.

Every night we are wrenched awake up to 30 times a night by horrific, blood-curdling screams. It has been like this every night for 21 months.

The only times my husband and I get any sleep is if we sleep away from home. My husband's mother's house is our respite care. We take turns sleeping there every now and then, when we just can't cope anymore. The soft pillows are a refuge from the horror down the road. We don't think about the one left home, coping alone with our son's wake-ups. It would be a waste of that person's ordeal for the other to stay up anxious during this rare chance for sleep. We pop a sleeping pill and black out until the morning.

Our eldest son also sees his nana's house as an escape. After a particularly bad week of wake-ups from his brother he will tell her direct: 'I need a sleepover, Nana'.

She has also taken the baby who will not sleep. The house felt so quiet without him. It was a delicious peek into a life that isn't ours. A life where night-time isn't to be dreaded. The guilt that followed those feelings tears at my heart still.

Whether he is in bed with us or in his cot or on the floor on the mattress by his cot he screams in the same way.

We have seen sleep consultants, of course we have. They have sat in our lounge as we tried to explain the screaming. Here, we said each time, you'll hear it in about five minutes. He wakes like clockwork. On cue the screams filled the lounge through the baby monitor.

They're always perplexed by the screaming.

Even when he's in bed with you and you're holding him he screams like that?

Yes. Even then. No matter where he is.

Pull his bedtime forward by half an hour. That's about the only thing you can do, as you're doing everything else.

We did. It didn't work.

Have you tried a chiropractor or an osteopath?

We tried the chiropractor. Five visits. It didn't work.

We did not try the osteopath or the healing crystals, though we did consider it. Which I think shows our desperation. We steadfastly refuse to consider whether past-life trauma is behind the screaming.

Have you tried just telling him to go to sleep?

Yes. It doesn't work.

We went back to the GP again and again and again. 'You don't understand', we said, pleading . . .

We are exhausted.

Please.

Help us.

The spiel is always the same. Babies don't sleep. As if our problem is just not understanding this simple fact and adjusting our lives accordingly. As if we haven't given up almost everything to function. As if our oldest son is an apparition and we are just first-time parents who expected our baby to sleep through from six weeks old.

And even if that were the case — can't we be treated with some empathy?

We are told to leave him to scream from 7 p.m. till 7 a.m. Shut the door. Don't go in. Put some towels in the cot for vomit. Bumpers for the crib if he bangs his head. This advice is repeated often.

Yeah, I'm not going to do that, I say.

When you're tired enough you will, the GP replies.

When you're tired enough is the chorus that surrounds us constantly. It is as relentless as the wake-ups in the night.

In another appointment, I sob and fall over my words. I want to tell the GP about being too tired to drive now. About the blurry vision I've been getting. The headaches. My husband's back. He is always sore.

She prescribes anti-depressants and I feel like a failure. I am too tired to remember to take them anyway.

We are constantly told to leave him to cry as if this is The Answer, and we're just too stupid to do it.

Smug faces spew out advice that we've heard a thousand times before.

Predatory sleep consultants want to be the ones that fix our child. They talk about him like he's a dog that just needs the right trainer. Like he's broken. When I turn them down gently their true colours show.

I guess you need material for your blog and if you got help for your child's sleep then you wouldn't have any.

The same sleep consultants post in mum groups encouraging people to train their three-week-old babies. They talk about 'respecting' your baby by teaching them to sleep.

A good mother would do this. A good mother would get her child sleeping through the night.

Posts about sleep on Facebook make me cry. Inevitably someone always turns up to the conversation as the wise old parent who has been there and done that.

We left them to cry — if you're tired enough you'll do it.

The co-sleepers want to claim me, though I hate co-sleeping and do it only out of necessity. But at least they're not as aggressive as the Cry It Out brigade. I feel more aligned with them, though I don't want to march under anybody's flag.

A new study came out about sleep training. It was sent to me dozens of times. Shared all over Facebook. I commented on one post, something I know I shouldn't do:

Unless you're in it, you don't really know what you'll do. And what works for one child likely won't work for another.

And then of course *when you're tired enough* comes again.

I've developed a tremor in my hand. I'm told it relates to exhaustion. People see me and say you don't look well.

Finally we get an appointment at the paediatrician. We get

tests. It's not behavioural — meaning we haven't caused this.

I feel like this should bring me relief. It's what we have wanted to hear for so long because it's such a tidy 'fuck you' to everyone who said *when you're tired enough*.

But it means nothing, because they still don't know how to get him to sleep.

We drug him under the orders of the paediatrician. For a blessed few days it works. Is this what life is like? Everything feels manageable. It's beautiful. We chase ducks. We have energy. We smile more.

Colour comes back to our cheeks. I finally shake the cold I've had for months. It is glorious.

After four days he becomes immune to the medication and he goes back to waking.

One night neither of us can physically get up. Suddenly the screaming stops and we hear crying.

I go into the room and my oldest son, just three years old, is standing on a chair he has pushed toward the cot.

He is holding tight to his brother over the bars of the cot. They cling to each other. Both are crying.

My oldest turns to me, shaking and unable to get the words out. Finally he says them with anger.

This is our baby.

He is furious and devastated. Fat tears are tumbling down his face and he puts out an angry hand at me, swatting at the darkness.

You are not kind.

Our baby was crying.

WHERE WAS YOU?

You are not kind.

This is our baby.

His words cut through. I lift our baby out of the cot and

hold my boys on my lap. My oldest slowly stops shaking, his breathing calms, but he will not let go of his baby brother's hand.

I'm sorry. Mama is just so tired. I couldn't wake up. I'm just too tired.

They each lay their heads against my chest. Our heartbeats slow and join.

This is our baby.

It's not going to change.

This is him. And we have to accept it.

We're tired enough now.

This is it.

The word I wish I could take back

BY GEM WILDER

Gem Wilder is a Wellington writer. She has performed and published work in a number of places, including Sport, Turbine | Kapohau, Common Ground Community Arts Festival, Kava Club Chop Suey Hui *and* TEZA 2015.

Motherhood comes with its own language. As soon as you find out you are pregnant, you acquire a whole new vocabulary: Antenatal, post-partum, meconium, placenta, nuchal fold, lactation and so on and so forth, forever and ever, amen. Some of these new words can inspire a plethora of emotions and memories. Words like 'latch' can bring on a cold sweat. My sympathies to you if you gave birth in a New Zealand election year, when every utterance of the word 'labour' can reduce you to a sobbing mess rocking on the floor, nothing but a bundle of PTSD and hormones.

There are words that come freely with motherhood that are suddenly easier to say than ever before. Words like 'I love you' and, more than that, 'I love you so so SO much, you make me so happy, come here so Mama can snuggle you to pieces.' Yep, you'll say these things, and you won't even gag when you do. You'll say them in public without an ounce of shame. You'll say them even as you are wiping your kid's snotty nose with your bare hands because you don't have any tissues, and you'll mean them sincerely.

You will understand a language that makes no sense outside of your small family unit. My family know that 'bawnmolly' was my nephew's word for lawnmower when he was a toddler. That 'donner' was the cord on the side of his sleep sack that he would wrap around his hand as he sucked his thumb. We know that when his younger brother asked for a 'cuggle' he wanted to suck on the side of his mother's thumb, her skin tough and dry from many a night spent soothing her boy. We know that when my daughter talks about 'pippit' she means cricket, and we laugh when she talks about how pippit players wear iPads. When my daughter pipes up from the back seat of the car, excited about having seen a 'pane,' I have to decipher whether she means plane, train or crane.

There are the words that people get wrong, like my daughter's name. People that have known her since she was born, who hear us pronounce Kōwhai with a long o, like core, still call her Kowhai with a short o, as if it doesn't matter how they say it. As if it is still her name if they pronounce it an entirely different way. I knew this would happen. I have no regrets when it comes to my daughter's name. She will tire of correcting people, or not. Maybe she won't care. Maybe her presence in the world will inspire a few more people to learn the correct pronunciation of the beautiful native tree she was named after.

There are the words we use as terms of affection for our child, the nicknames she endures. My bunny baby, kokomo, koko pops, my only sunshine. And the words she uses to define us, her parents. Mama. Papa. Titles we earned and owned the second she took her first breath.

My daughter is three and a half now, a chatterbox with a growing vocabulary. I hear her mimicking me often. I hear her testing out new words to see how they feel on her tongue. A few weeks ago she was describing an incident that had happened to her at daycare. 'I was feeling . . .' and she paused, thinking of the right word to describe her emotion, '. . . *frustrated*,' she finished, confident that she'd used this new word correctly.

All of these words I treasure. I wouldn't take back a single one of them. Except . . . there is one word that I have overused during my time as a mama, and that word is 'careful.'

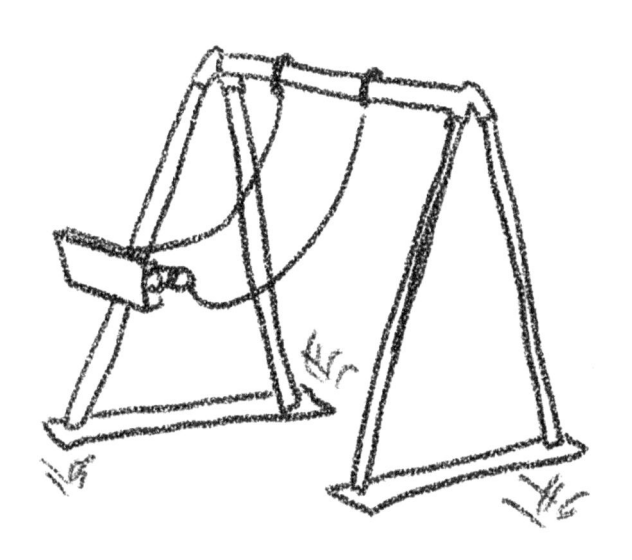

I utter it numerous times a day. When my daughter is climbing along the top of the couch, when she is carrying a glass of water, when we're out walking, when she's playing rough and tumble with her cousins, when she's curiously stroking a baby, when she's climbing out of the bath. I say it, and then I see it. I see my daughter being careful. I see her playing at a playground and avoiding ladders she thinks she cannot climb. I see her wary of the touch pool at the aquarium, standing in such a way that she can look at the starfish with no risk of getting her hands wet. I see her being careful, being cautious, being wary.

Careful is the word I have used the most since becoming a mother, and I hate it. I don't want it to be the word that defines my motherhood. If I could start over I would tell my daughter to have fun. I would let her learn for herself what she is capable of, before planting the seed of danger or failure before she's even tried something. When I told her to be careful I did so out of love, but also out of fear.

I've learnt my lesson, though, and these days I sound like a cheerleader, or a motivational poster. 'You can do it!' I call from the sidelines. 'Just try it!' I plead. And hopefully, if I keep this up, before too long she will start to believe me. If I say it out loud enough times, maybe that's what she'll start hearing inside her own head.

10 parenting styles that are definitely a thing and aren't made up

BY EMILY WRITES

What's your parenting style? Are you an attachment parent? A helicopter parent? A free-range parent? An authoritative parent? An evolutionary parent? A paleo parent? A tiger parent?

Ahhh, parenting philosophies! It seems these days everyone has one. A guiding set of principles can be great — and thankfully there are heaps of different ways to parent. I was kind of into attachment parenting but I don't like being around my children that much. I'm too lazy to be a helicopter parent. I could be a free-range parent because I have white privilege, which means if I just let my kids roam the neighbourhood I can blog about it ad nauseum without having to consider why I'm able to do this while other mothers can't. Evolutionary parenting? Well, it sounds appealing. If it was good enough for a cave-mum with a life expectancy of 22 it's good enough for this millennial.

In short, I'm on the hunt for a philosophy that works for me. Here are 10 new philosophies that are sure to be written about in *Time* magazine in two years:

1. CAN YOU JUST NOT? MAMA IS REALLY TIRED PARENTING

This parenting style involves laying on the couch while your children draw on the walls and climb all over you. It involves moaning 'ughhh, go play trains' every five minutes or so. It's great for teaching independence, because it's important that children learn to be content and happy in their own company. Can You Just Not? Mama Is Really Tired parents tend to have children who are non-sleepers. That's why they're Can You Just Not? Mama Is Really Tired parents in the first place.

2. MAMA IS ON THE PHONE I SAID I'M ON THE PHONE PARENTING

Is there any greater joy than being a stay-at-home parent but also having to work otherwise you can't afford groceries? A growing group of mothers who are working stay-at-home parents are turning to Mama Is On The Phone I SAID I'M ON THE PHONE parenting so they can truly have it all! This style of parenting involves apologising profusely to the person you're talking to on the phone, asking clients and people you're interviewing to 'Please can you repeat that?', saying 'No honestly, it's fine, now is a good time' six to eight times a day, and reassuring people that your children aren't murdering each other. This parenting philosophy also includes a weak smile to give to other parents who say 'You're so lucky you get the best of both worlds!'

3. CUCUMBER PARENTING

You know your child will eat cucumber and it's at least healthy so it's OK if they eat an entire cucumber and nothing else in a day. Everything will be fine. Honestly. Cucumbers are super healthy and probably have heaps of nutrients (just don't Google it). This type of parenting is defined by doing the best you can within the limits of your child's ridiculous and frankly fucking batshit quirks. So they want to wear a snowsuit with a beanie, gloves, two pairs of socks and a scarf when it's 24 degrees? Let them. Cucumber kids learn that their choices are not always good ones. Plus, cucumber is mostly water so they'll hydrate while they're sweating and insisting that they're not too hot.

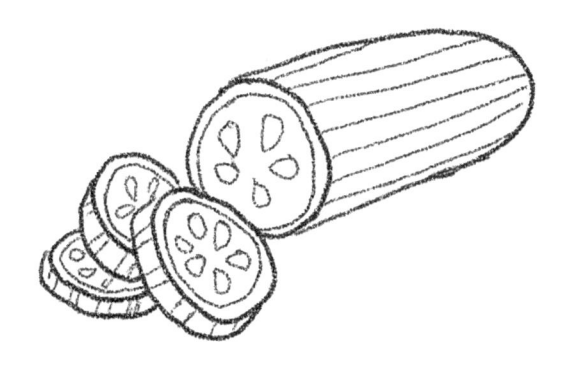

4. PINOCCHIO PARENTING

The other day I said to another mother, 'Yeah, same, totally, I don't let my kids eat McDonald's either', while my child's face was covered in sweet and sour sauce and he was holding a chicken nugget. This is Pinocchio parenting. It's a must for insecure parents with anxiety — lying about how you parent is a great life-hack. I don't ever give my child juice. I limit screen time. And my child totally sleeps through the night! My oldest has been out of nappies since he was two.

My youngest just asked me if he could have a nap — in three different languages! You too can be a perfect parent if you just lie about everything.

5. INSTAGRAM PARENTING

Where you lock your children in a crate so you can get your lounge clean enough for the perfect Flat Lay.

6. CAPYBARA PARENTING

You've heard of tiger parenting and dolphin parenting? Well, capybara parenting is all the rage now. Capybaras are chill as fuck — they're like little wine barrels on legs. They live with other mum capybaras and they just hang out eating and sleeping and watching each other's kids. All the baby capybaras are looked after by whichever mum has the most energy. When one mum capybara is tired, or if her second glass of wine was a heavy pour, the other capybara mums just look after her child or put on some *Peppa Pig* or something. Or they build a fort and say to the kids, 'Let's play a game called "how long you can stay quiet and not break anything while the mummies are on the deck".' They don't judge each other when their baby capybaras are being feral. They just chill and are like, 'Do you want some more cake? Is your cider OK? Girl, your hair is so good, can you henna mine?'

7. ON DISPLAY PARENTING

When you're at Chipmunks and you say to your child, 'See that camera? It's a whingeing camera and it can detect whingeing. If you keep whingeing at me, the camera will alert the whingeing security team and they'll come over and we'll have to leave and we'll never be able to come back. I'll probably get sent to jail.' And then another mother comes over and you quickly say, 'Thank you for expressing yourself! I see you! I hear you! I validate your feelings! Let's count to ten and take some deep breaths and then maybe you can have a fruit cup. We love to share, don't we! Mummy loves you!'

8. ONCE A WEEK MUSIC CLASS PARENTING

Once A Week Music Class parenting is when you can justify letting your child watch 18 hours of *Paw Patrol* because you took them to that dire music class where everyone knew each other but you didn't know anyone and you forgot to bring a donation and you didn't know the actions to any of the songs and your child just lay on the ground screaming anyway until they shit their pants and you realised you forgot to put wipes in the nappy bag.

9. OH, THATS NOT MY CHILD PARENTING

This is when someone comes up to you and says, 'Excuse me is that your child over there?' and points to the kid who has buried himself up to his neck in the sandpit and is now calling all the other kids in the playground fascists and you say 'Oh, that's not my child' and go back to your phone.

10. CUB SCOUT PARENTING

When I was a kid I went to Scouts. The leader would say 'Cubs do your best!' and we would shout 'We will do our best!' It was a rally cry and a promise. One that suits parenting. We make promises when we make a family. To our children, to ourselves, to our partners, to our families. We promise to do our best. Not *the* best. Just our best. We promise to love and care for our babies and we promise to try. Some days are so long and hard and we struggle to understand this as our babies grow so fast before our eyes. How is it that we carry them one day and the next they say, 'I can walk, Mama'? We close our eyes and count or we take a deep breath and smile when they're screaming 'YOU ARE NOT MY BEST FRIEND!' When precious things are broken we keep perspective because our most precious things aren't broken. We stand in the doorways of nurseries and bedrooms smiling and sighing, we lay on the floor by cots with tiny hands wrapped around our fingers as we hum lullabies. As the night falls and we keep on parenting we whisper thanks for all that we have. We do our best. Sometimes our best doesn't feel like it's good enough. But it is. And we keep doing our best. Every day. For the best things that have happened to us, we do our best.

'Today, I'm going back on my antidepressants:' A stay-at-home mum on tackling depression

BY JULIA KERR

Julia Kerr is a wife, mother and stay-at-home hero, getting by on hot coffee and tiny hugs. Her interests include sharing stories, normalising parenthood and searching for wine.

I weaned myself off anti-depressants about 18 months ago. After six years, I wanted to see if I was able to manage my depression naturally. I was in a safe and happy place in my life and trusted that I would have all of the support I needed to help me on that journey.

I have been mindful of my diet, I have kept moving and I've made sure I get fresh air and sunshine. In the lead-up to coming off my anti-depressants, I kept good track of my emotions and my triggers. I took note of how I felt at different times and how different things affected me. This time has been crucial in understanding how my head works and what I can do to manage it. I feel like I know myself really well now and that's really important to me.

And that's also why I have chosen to go back on my medication.

For the most part, life has been really good. Day to day, I can't really complain outside the usual stresses of family life. I'm mostly happy.

But man, I'm tired.

Despite my best efforts, I still have those rough days. I still wake up some mornings with my head on a little crooked, feeling like I'm pinned to my bed. I still feel the walls closing in and I know I need to get out of the house, but I can't bring myself to do it. I still lose my patience and get so angry with my kids and that's not fair. I can't explain what it feels like when you are shouting at your children, knowing you should stop but you feel unable to because anger is a side-effect of your depression.

I have to work really hard to remind myself that it's not permanent, these feelings will pass and I'm still a good person. But I also have to really fight to keep my head above water. I have to fight to remember that I'm worth something and that I mean something to other people. During these times, I struggle to remember that I have value in the world.

And I'm just over it.

Though these really bad patches are few and far between, I still feel like I'm facing little struggles every day. Things that maybe don't need to be the way they are. Things that cause me to overthink and drain my energy without me even realising it. When I take something out of context, when I'm not able to make decisions or recall details — that's my depression.

A major and ongoing part of my illness is memory loss. This is the biggest battle I face every day because it makes me unreliable, and as a mother (to me) that's something I just can't be.

Increasingly, I feel like I'm spending a lot of energy fighting a battle that just doesn't need to be fought. I know now that I *can* live without my medication but I have a war in my mind.

Can you imagine that? Can you imagine what it's like to try to parent when it takes you 10 minutes just to get the milk out of the fridge? Or how it feels to convince yourself your husband is going to leave you because why the fuck would he want you anyway? Or how truly crazy you feel when you suddenly develop an irrational fear of cleaning the oven or listening to female vocalists or using steel forks in ceramic bowls or anything else that's equally ridiculous but is very, very real to you?

I want to make things easier for myself.

So today, I'm going back on my anti-depressants. While I know this doesn't 'cure' my depression or 'fix' my anxiety, it does help me manage it. It helps me conserve my energy for more important things.

I know I will still have good days and bad days; I will still get stressed and I will still feel anxious and frustrated at times because I'm alive and that's normal.

But this helps me see things for what they truly are. It will help me realise that driving somewhere unfamiliar isn't actually as scary as my head tells me it is, or that I won't actually die if I get stuck in a crowd. When I'm trapped under my blankets because I've woken up in a world where shit is bad and no one likes me, it will help me to hold onto the idea that the world is good and I'll be OK soon.

Depression is not an emotion. It's not a mood.

Anxiety is not just a feeling. It's an illness that I'm treating.

I'm not going to deny my family the best version of myself because of the stigma that comes with being medicated. Not everyone has to understand or agree with my choice, but I don't care about that because not everyone can understand mental illness. Medication might not work for everyone, but it does work for some. It's taken me a fair amount of trial and error, but I've found something that works for me and that is what's important.

I know I can be better. I don't want to hold myself back with negative thinking and self-doubt. I want to feel motivated again. I want to be, do and achieve as much as I am able to, and if I need medication to help me accomplish that, then that's OK.

Are mum groups on Facebook a vortex to hell?

BY EMILY WRITES

I saw *Blade Runner 2049* finally. Without much of an interest in blades or running, it took me a while. I saw it only because it has Ryan 'Sad Eyes' Gosling in it. As I was watching, I thought about how I would report back to one of the only groups I'm in on Facebook. It's not a mum group. It's a collective of, well . . . mostly mums and some gay dudes — anyone with an appreciation for proper reviewing of movies (as in, don't waste your time seeing a movie that somehow doesn't have Zac Efron in a shower in it). It is aptly named 'The Zac Efron Shower Scene Rom Com Appreciation Club'.

I started this group after being repeatedly asked to set up a mum group on Facebook. These days most mummy bloggers have a companion 'group' that goes with their blog. This to me, and I mean this with all respect, sounds like an unending nightmare.

Don't get me wrong, mum groups can be a wonderful place for support and guidance. But they can also be, how can I put this . . . a vortex to hell? And I would like to not have to moderate a group of thousands of sleep-deprived people fighting over forward-facing car seats and sleep training.

I admire the resilience of anyone moderating and being an admin in a Facebook group. I have been an admin before for a very large group — and it's for that reason that I'm no longer a member of any of these large groups. I don't know what makes Facebook groups such toxic places for parents, but many of them are horrific. And some admins don't have the time or energy or maybe even the inclination to handle them (that 'all drama is engagement and engagement means more likes and more likes means free shit' thing).

Some have tried to nail down the 'no judgement' rules. Some have somehow gone too far and ended up with posts where mothers support a parent who shaved off her daughter's hair because her daughter didn't listen to her (yes, this happened).

All in all, my mental health has been a heck of a lot better since I left all of these groups and stopped seeing parents screaming at each other for hours at a time over whether it's OK to use a Bumbo. For at least six months I haven't been subjected to: 'OK, so I know I could ask a doctor, but instead I'm going to ask 8000 parents living on one hour of sleep: should I vaccinate?' or *posts photos of baby with half a leg* 'do you think I should take my baby into A&E? Her leg just fell off'.

I have not seen a rash post in so long — I am truly #blessed.

When I first became a mother I joined every mum group I could find. I had no idea what I was doing and I wanted to know. I wanted guidance and help. I wanted to be able to say 'Is this normal?' I wanted a community.

I have found this in Facebook groups — but not in Facebook mum groups.

In the Facebook mum groups I was in I became fixated on feeding because it was all anyone talked about. I started to feel I was going mad. Post after post was on mixed feeding and bottles and nipple creams and mastitis. Studies and studies and studies on how breastfeeding didn't matter (not great when you're trying to breastfeed and you're being told 'you don't even know what's in breast milk/your baby will starve') and studies and studies and studies on how formula feeding is bad for your baby (not great when you're trying to formula feed and keep being told your baby will have 'a low IQ and no immune system').

My second time with a new baby, and not in any of these groups, I actually went and sought face-to-face advice and guidance on feeding. I felt so much less anxious. I let go of the baggage I had from my first baby and had a far healthier mindset toward feeding — leaving me and my baby a lot happier. (I did bitch a lot on Twitter about it — but Twitter has a great group of Twitter parents who you can totally moan about feeding to without any of them accusing you of hating breastfeeding/formula-feeding mums because you have asked for help).

I had a sick baby the first time around, and the competitive nature of mum groups only highlighted that he was underweight and not meeting milestones. The relentless health privilege in many mum groups was exhausting. My son was on heavy, heavy drugs to keep him alive in ICU when I read a mother's screed on how she would never give her child any Pamol because it's all poison. Modern medicine was 'unneeded'. Vaccination killed, and any child who died from a preventable disease was a case of 'survival of the fittest'. Everything was Big Pharma or Big Hospital or, I shit you not, 'Big Obstetrician'. Or 'Have you tried a cranial osteopath for your child's kidney disorder? It totally works!' Don't even get me started on how often people told me to try amber beads when my son was in hospital with a tracheal collapse.

Competiparents humble-bragged about their kids constantly. 'My six-week-old is ready for school. How can I slow down how advanced she is?'

The groups were so white it was painful. 'Why can't I have golliwogs? This is PC gone mad! Next you'll tell me I can't have my *Little Black Sambo* book!'

Sleep — dear lord! 'Don't hate me because my child is having 125 hours of sleep a night! It's actually really hard!', 'Just because my child is getting 24 hours sleep a night it doesn't mean I am!' or 'I sleep train because I respect and love my baby — not saying you don't, but maybe you shouldn't have had kids', 'No judgement, but my child sleeps so much I've forgotten their name', 'Not an ad but if you mention my name you get 20 per cent off at Baby Sleep Consultants R Us'.

And everything, *everything*, turned into a fight. And I joined in. I remember the day I quit cold turkey — I realised I was having an argument with a mum about toothpaste. I don't know how it happened.

So many groups just foster this atmosphere of tension and justification. You're so rarked up all the time because so many of the posts are passive-aggressive or straight-out aggressive-aggressive (is that a thing?) And you're exhausted and overwhelmed and frankly a bit rusty with socialisation given you're stuck at home a lot . . . it's possibly inevitable.

So I quit.

And instead I joined groups that made me feel empowered as a mother. I joined smaller groups — we all knew each other so we were kind to each other and gave each other the benefit of the doubt. We were still able to be 'social' even though we were locked inside with sick kids. We gently challenged each other on comments that were unintentionally hurtful **SO WE COULD LEARN** (amazing!).

I love now being around people who know feeding isn't the be-all and end-all that we thought it was. We don't fixate on milestones — we celebrate our children as unique. We know sleep happens when it happens; we cheer each other up when it has been a bad night and we celebrate the good nights. We don't give unsolicited advice or free advertising for sleep consultants. We know we have more in common than we think when it comes to parenting and we know exhaustion makes it very, very, very hard to connect with others, so we are gentle.

So if you've found your group, hold on tight.

Love those women like they're your sisters. Find your village and set up camp.

The best group I've ever been part of is a lovely, kind, caring, diverse and supportive community of (brilliant and amazing) mothers where we talk about things outside of parenting without making parenting seem like something we can't talk about. It has helped me in so many ways. And the ZESSRCAC is a thirsty delight — we never talk about kids unless it's to complain that *Married At First Sight* is on and they need to go the fuck to sleep. I'm also in a few PND and anxiety groups to support others after having that same support given to me when I was struggling.

So, clearly, Facebook groups aren't a vortex to hell. But they can put you in a bad place, just as they can take you to a much better place as a parent. You just need to work out where your group is taking you, and if that's where you want to go.

My babies don't move: A story of physio, growth charts and slow walkers

BY JULIET SPEEDY

Juliet Speedy is a Christchurch-based journalist and writer who juggles her time between newsrooms, supermarkets, kindy, the library and the laundry. She has three small kids who were born closer together than she can remember.

My third child was one year and one week old when he started crawling. I rang my Mum. 'Mum! I have an early mover. A baby that moves! What do I do with him?' She laughed. We both laughed that many parents around the world would be stressed if their baby wasn't walking by this age, let alone had only just started crawling. But not me, no daddy-o. My babies don't move. My now six- and four-year-old children both started walking when they were just shy of 20 months old — outside of all of the graphs, charts and realm that experts consider 'normal'.

'Your baby will start walking around 12 months,' screamed up at me from every piece of literature I ever read.

'Some as late as 16–18 months,' also appeared.

'Anything outside of that, see the professionals,' I often read.

Neither of my eldest children was crawling at 12 months. Neither of them was moving at all. In fact, they had not long learnt to sit up. My eldest could barely weight-bear. Actually, at 12 months old he wasn't. So Plunket referred me to the hospital when he was 13 months old. From there we had blood tests, scans, x-rays and paediatrician appointments.

I'll never forget the day when, sitting in the paediatrician's office with my 13-month-old first-born eating raisins on her floor, the serious-faced doctor said: 'It may be nothing or it could be something more serious like cerebral palsy.'

The walls of her office started spinning.

I was no paediatrician, but I felt pretty sure I'd have known if my round-faced little baby had cerebral palsy.

It wasn't just the experts. 'Is he still not walking yet?' I often heard.

'You know, there are places you can go for that,' I was advised.

'Wow, you must be so worried,' said one, who appeared to be more worried than me.

Should I have been worried? I Googled: '15 month old still not walking'. I just seemed to find chat rooms of mums advising each other on what was and wasn't normal. I stopped reading them as soon as I'd started.

My baby was then referred to a physiotherapist. For nine months we had a physio visit our home every fortnight to play with my boy and me in an effort to encourage him to move.

'For some babies, it's like maths,' said the physio. 'Some just need a bit more help than others.'

Eventually he started to crawl, and then to walk.

In his own time.

The physio admitted that she had been worried about him when she first came. Now he was walking, she wasn't. 'You're discharged,' she said to him. He smiled and toddled off.

Just four weeks later his sister arrived. That was lucky. I didn't really want to have to carry both a toddler and a newborn out to the car every time we left the house.

Twelve months later my daughter turned one. She wasn't moving. Plunket was concerned. 'I think we should refer her to a physio.'

'OK,' I agreed half-heartedly. 'I'm sure she'll get there in her own time. Our babies don't seem to move.' But physio she had.

Eventually she bum-shuffled around the floor for a few months, crawled for a bit and then at 19 months, two weeks before her little brother arrived on the scene, she started to walk. That was lucky. I didn't really want to have to carry both a toddler and a newborn out to the car every time we left the house.

With friends and family, we laughed. With our last name being Speedy, the irony was not lost: 'Another Speedy baby who's not so speedy.'

Baby number three was another handsome little boy. He was going to be no different, I was sure. Actually, I hoped he wasn't. An immobile baby is much less work for a mother of three. Now I had a tribe, having one sit on his butt and not wreak havoc was actually a godsend.

It's nothing but interesting that all three have been slow off the mark. Is it genes? We joke about which side of the family is to blame. 'I was a lazy baby,' said my mum. My hubby's dad couldn't find his Plunket books.

I have, of course, heard many theories from many people along the way.

Have you not given them enough tummy time?

It's because your babies have such big heads.

He's an early talker, his brain is too busy focusing on that.

When our number three was nine months old, our new lovely Plunket nurse said, 'He's still not moving, is he? I think we should refer him to physio.'

'Are you sure we need to yet?' I queried. 'Our babies don't move.'

The postscript is that my six-year-old is now playing rugby and cricket, riding a skateboard and running faster than me. My four-year-old spends hours daily dancing to Spotify on our kitchen floor. My two-year-old is joining in on all of it.

Our babies didn't fit into the charts of 'normal' but to me, that's a badge of honour. I love that they're different. I never bake biscuits with cookie cutters anyway.

How to survive severe sleep deprivation — by someone who is living it

BY EMILY WRITES

Having not slept for 800 years, I feel somewhat qualified to talk about surviving severe sleep deprivation. For more than a year I (barely) survived on about three hours sleep, broken throughout the night. Now I get around five hours — often three hours in a row. I've had a handful of nights where I've slept all night, when I've been away from my youngest.

So I thought it might be useful to share some tips on how to get through it. They won't work for everyone, they won't all work, but some will, for some people. They work for me — and they're the reason why I've been able to get through the past four years.

Before any sleep consultants target me for glamourising sleep deprivation, I'd like to point out that I'm writing this from my sick bed. I smell . . . not good. Not bad. But not good. I haven't brushed my hair in a while. I am wearing my husband's old Motorhead t-shirt and a pair of boxers, and when I go to kindy pick-up I'm just going to put on my 'looks a bit like pants but are actually PJs'.

I am not glamorous. Sleep deprivation isn't glamorous. Even if I wanted to seem glamorous, I couldn't.

I only share stuff about sleep because 1) I am told it helps other mums who are trying to parent on not enough sleep and 2) I'm living it, so what the hell else am I going to write about? If you don't sleep, it's all you think about. I try to write about other stuff but it all comes back to sleep.

I don't write about sleep to glamourise not getting it. I do take the point though that I'm normalising sleep deprivation.

I am normalising it . . . because . . . wait for it . . . it's normal.

Babies do, and are totally meant to, wake frequently. They wake frequently for a number of reasons — they're hungry, wet, cold, they exist in the world, they are upset that they don't have enough hair, they had a dream where they got put in a pelican's mouth . . . the list goes on.

Sometimes we know the reasons why they wake up, but often we have no idea. And this also is totally normal.

I'm sorry if that doesn't work with your business model, but it's the truth.

This *points to black bags under eyes* is normal.

Normal doesn't mean it's pleasant. Normal doesn't mean it's fun. It's awful and it's hard — and if you've ever thought 'what kind of mother would I be if my kid just fucking slept?', know that I think this all the time. You're not alone.

You are not a bad mother for having a child who doesn't sleep. Your child isn't broken. They're not a problem that needs to be fixed. You don't have to be fixed.

It's just a reality of parenting for a lot of mums. And they're the mums I'm writing to now.

All babies are different. Some babies sleep well and easily from an early age. Some do not. There are no tricks or secrets.

These truths don't sit well with the sleep-training industry because they make it harder to sell products and services to mums. So, before we get stuck in, to any sleep consultants who are reading and are already pissed off — let me just say this: I am a mum who is just doing her best and you don't have to read further. If you like, you could just go and watch some TV. I recommend *GLOW*, it's really great. It's about women's wrestling but also about friendships and it has a killer soundtrack.

Are they gone? Good.

Let's just crack into it.

GET GOOD AT NAPPING

Four years into this lark, I'm the queen of napping. You need to learn how to nap. When my husband takes the kids to the park — I nap. When my kids fall asleep at the same time — I nap. When my mother-in-law takes them to lunch — I nap. I nap whenever I can. I nap in the hour between coming home from work and eating dinner. I nap in the morning after I drop them at kindy before I start my day. I nap at the same time they do. I choose naps over everything else — *everything* else.

I wasn't always good at napping — I would lay down and check Facebook or start a mental list in my head of all of the things I had to do. I would fixate on the time I had: 'only half an hour — not long enough for a nap'. Now I know even 20 minutes is long enough for a nap.

When my husband says, 'I'll take over, have a nap', I'm asleep before he even finishes the sentence.

My tip is to take every single opportunity to lie down. Change into PJs even if you don't have much time; I reckon it tells your brain it's sleep time. I'm not a scientist, though — I was drunk through most of my final years of school. Put your phone away.

Lie with your eyes closed and try to clear your mind. It takes a while to train your brain to nap at every opportunity but you will get there. The key is not to waste any time thinking about anything else or looking at your phone. Social media kills naps — get rid of it. And even if you only nap for 10 minutes, it's worth it.

Napping has never stopped me being able to sleep at night, but that's because I'm severely sleep deprived. It will be the same for you if you're running on four hours or so. If you're getting seven plus, taking a nap might be counter-productive, as it might stop you being able to sleep at night.

GO TO BED EARLY

I know. Boring as shit. You want to see your partner, if you have one. You want to see friends. You want to zone out in front of the TV. I get it. But schedule at least one night a week when you go to bed with your child — whether it's falling asleep with them at 7 p.m. or going into your own bed once you get them down. At least once a week, preferably on the same day, you need to go to bed at 7 p.m. I do this a couple of times a week.

LEAVE THE CLEANING OR DROP YOUR STANDARDS

This is obviously harder if you find mess to be anxiety-inducing. I understand how a clean kitchen can make you feel better when everything else feels overwhelming. So you do you. But we have severely dropped our standards around chores. I don't fold washing anymore; the kids' clothes get shoved into the drawers. There's clutter everywhere — and I plan on dealing with it as soon as my kid sleeps through the night. We never clear the laundry pile, it is just replaced constantly. We have decided naps and rest are more important at the moment. If the house is too messy, we leave the house. This is only going to be the case for the next, like, year or so.

IF YOU HAVE A PARTNER, MAKE SURE THEY'RE NOT A DICK

If you have a partner, make sure they understand that they're also a parent. Whether your partner works outside the home or not, they should be getting up through the night too, or doing shifts with you so you get sleep. My husband and I split the night — one of us goes to bed early so they can get up early and the other wakes up to the baby in the night, but sleeps in. We give each other naps and touch base every morning and night to see how we are doing. If one of us is about to hit a wall, we take turns around who needs the spare bed. There are nights my husband needs a whole night, and nights I do, but we completely share getting up to the kids because we are both parents.

A friend told me her husband said he worked so he couldn't ever get up. They're divorced now, which I think is great. Because only fucking dicks say shit like that. This is one of the most common things I hear from sleep-deprived mums — that their partners don't get up because they 'work'. We all work. Home or office — it's work. So dads: do the right thing. Get up. You're tired? Suck it up — that's being a parent. We are all tired.

BANG AS OFTEN AS IS HUMANLY POSSIBLE

I know it's the last thing you feel like doing. But if you are with someone who is good at banging, banging will do you both a world of good. If you're not — rub one out/flick ya bean. It will help you sleep and you'll have a better and deeper sleep. And if it's with the other person you're parenting with, it'll help you connect when it feels like you're just flatmates. I would never turn down a good knobbing and I recommend the same for you.

CALL THE VILLAGE

Ring friends or family and ask for help. Asking for help is really hard — but you need to do it. When I wasn't coping, I asked my friends for help and we set up a roster for one morning a week for them to take my kids to Chipmunks. We share the load when we can and drop off food. We've tried to make a culture of helping each other out.

When someone offers you food or babysitting, accept it. (I mean, provided they're not a psychopath incapable of looking after children, obviously.) For some reason it's a gut reaction to reject help. Try to change that mindset and accept any help that comes your way.

THIS IS VERY SPECIFIC, BUT PUT ON DARK GLASSES AND GO TO SLEEP UNDERNEATH THEM DURING YOUR CHILD'S SWIMMING LESSON OR GYMNASTICS CLASS

Trust me, they won't notice. And it's not like they're going to suddenly learn how to do a forward roll after 15 fucking terms.

GIVE NO FUCKS

This is probably the most important. Give no fucks about what people think of your parenting at night. You know your baby and you know what's best for them. If you want to cry, cry. If you want to scream, scream. I have stood on my balcony and literally yelled at a tree because I'm so upset and angry about not getting sleep. It's OK to feel upset that your life has been hijacked by lack of sleep. You can feel all of those things and still know in your heart that you're doing the right thing by your kids in whatever way you're helping them get to sleep. I know people tell you what to do, I know you hear 'have you tried . . . ?' a trillion times a day. I know it's hard. Give no fucks, my friend.

You are doing an awesome job. Whether your child sleeps 45 minutes a night or 11 hours is not a measure of how good you are at parenting. It says nothing about you as a mother.

Remember, there are no tricks. No secrets. You don't have to buy anything. You just have to give no fucks and remember you're a badass of epic proportions who gets through every day even though you get no sleep.

You're brilliant. You're amazing. And imagine how much shit you're going to get done when you do get sleep! I mean, look at you now — if you can be this awesome on two hours, you're going to change the world on six.

Remember: it will get better.

I promise.

Meats, shoots and leaves — A mum finds peace with what her child eats

BY LEAH HAMILTON

Leah Hamilton is a freelance writer and mother of two living in Berlin. She spends her days thinking about climate change and sustainable development, computer games, and which wine would pair best with a screaming child.

During my pregnancy with my first child, the main things I thought about in relation to introducing solids were that I didn't want her to be a picky eater. I also wanted to video her when she first ate lemon. I somehow mentally bypassed the fact that my husband and I ate primarily vegan food and had decided to eliminate meat from our diets at home for a multitude of reasons. This would (of course) affect the food we had in the house and what we would feed our daughter.

When we were ready to start solids, I felt bombarded by information from all sorts of places. I had heard that baby rice was not so good, baby-led weaning was the way to go, and that it was best if I made my own baby food at home. I had also heard that baby rice was extremely important, baby-led weaning would cause my daughter to choke, and that the squeezy baby-food pouches were lifesavers. I thought 'I can't possibly raise this baby to be vegan', and having her best interests at heart I dutifully went out and bought some beef and chicken. Every time I bought meat, I felt weird. Why was I buying something for my daughter that I would not eat myself? I definitely didn't want to be one of those vegans who ends up in the news for only feeding their child soy milk and buckwheat, but I also didn't want to make choices that I didn't feel were ethically right for our family.

So I did some research (thanks Dr Google!), talked to Plunket, talked to our GP (thanks Dr Doctor!), and decided with my husband that we would find a middle ground and raise our daughter to be a vegetarian. We figured that with cheese and yoghurt she wouldn't miss out on calcium, fat or B12, and with other nutrients coming from eggs, grains, pulses and fruit and vegetables, she would be fine.

Initially this wasn't a big deal: she couldn't talk, she ate pretty much whatever was put in front of her and she was too young to question which foods we eat and which foods we don't. She's nearly two and a half now and has started to show a greater interest in what we are eating and where it comes from, which has at times proved to be a little complicated.

We told her that almond milk and soy milk come from plants, while cow's milk comes from a cow. Every time she drinks cow's milk, she says, 'Thank you, cow!', and it's very adorable.

But then 20 minutes later I find myself saying, 'Just because we eat plants, it doesn't mean you should eat all plants. Please put that random berry back outside and don't eat it because it could make you very sick', and 'Evelyn! Did you bite this leaf off the capsicum plant?'

So we soldier on and keep trying to teach her about our diet and why we don't eat animals. But it's a bit harder to explain, 'When you eat meat, the animal that it came from ... dies. It's dead like that bird you saw outside and poked with a stick yesterday.' She listens carefully and says something like, 'Makes cow sad! I don't want cow be sad. I don't eat meat!', and I think, 'Yes, I have done such a great job today.' And then at Playcentre the next day somebody offers her a piece of sausage and she eats it. At that point there's nothing I can do other than to remind her gently that sausages are made from animals (and not even the good bits!), and that if she doesn't want to eat animals she shouldn't eat the sausage next time.

I've been asked, 'Don't you think it's wrong to force your vegetarian beliefs on your children?' No, I don't. It's my job as a parent to teach my children to behave how I think is right, which for us includes not eating animals, not hitting other kids, not eating lollies all day, being kind to other people and cleaning up after ourselves. She will still make her own choices and have her own preferences ('I don't pick up Duplo! Daddy do it!'), but it's my duty to try to teach her what I think is right and wrong, and provide her with relevant, truthful information. She can make her own informed choices when she is older, but for now, much like I don't let her eat lollies all day, I also don't cook meat for her anymore, and I do insist that she pick up her own Duplo.

Of course we also get the questions of 'What about iron? What about protein? Is that even healthy?' Contrary to popular belief, vegetarian diets are not 90 per cent lettuce, they're not deficient in protein, and iron is pretty easy to come by. You can find it in beans, lentils, chickpeas, leafy greens and even Marmite. There's always vitamin liquid too, if I'm worried we've been living off too many quesadillas and not enough 'healthy' food.

Now that a couple of years have gone by and my second child is about to start solids, I feel increasingly confident that our kids are going to grow up happy and healthy without meat. I'm even starting to field more questions like 'Can you give me some vegetarian recipes?' and 'Would you like this vegan lasagne?', rather than 'Do you really think that's good for your children?'

I think we have a long way to go before vegetarian children are considered to be normal rather than weirdos, especially in New Zealand where meat and dairy reign upon high, but at the very least I no longer feel like some hippy or neglectful parent for deciding to raise my family in the way I think is right for us.

The next step for me is making sure my daughter understands the difference between radishes, horseradish and horses. For goodness' sake, it's been 40 minutes. Just eat your damn potato salad already and stop saying 'neigh'.

'I didn't know who was failing — me or him': On having a child who can't read

BY NADINE ANNE HURA

Nadine Anne Hura (Ngāti Hine, Ngāpuhi) writes policy by day and essays by night. Her writing explores themes of identity, biculturalism, politics and parenting.

When I was five I learnt to read. Each letter had a name and a sound. When you lined the letters up and ran the sounds together, just like magic, you could hear yourself reading. It was incredibly simple.

So it came as a shock to me when my own son, at the age of five, couldn't do this. The shapes of letters made no sense to him; he had no idea how to decode them, and he didn't really care. He could read by rote, committing stories to memory after hearing them just once or twice. As far as he was concerned, it didn't matter which way up he held a book, because pictures looked good from all angles.

For the first two years of his schooling, I repeatedly asked my boy's teachers for help. They looked at me with knowing eyes ('pushy parent') and reassured me that boys take longer to learn to read than girls.

'Relax,' they all said. 'He'll read when he's ready.' A few months later they changed their tune. Suddenly, it was me who was in the gun. What had we been doing at home? Or, more to the point, what hadn't we been doing? Did we know our boy couldn't read? Didn't we realise that he attempted to read books upside down?

There was a sudden flurry of activity. Reading Recovery. A range of jaw-droppingly expensive tests. He was prescribed glasses and tracking exercises for his eyes. We booked a dyslexia assessment, the Holy Grail in the quest to understand the precise nature of my child's learning disorder. As I waited for the results, my hope that my boy was 'normal' wrestled with my hope that he wasn't. Having a label would be an advantage. Schools can work with labels. There'd be support. He'd qualify for extra time during exams.

But the tests were inconclusive. His wide vocabulary and his capacity for comprehension didn't square with the fact that he read words back to front, often missing out whole sentences without affecting his understanding. When the Brain Gym specialist held up a 3D block in the shape of a 'p' and asked what letter she was holding up my boy replied, 'The letter p'. When she turned it upside down so it resembled the shape of a 'd' and asked him again, he raised a suspicious eyebrow and said: 'The letter p. You're just holding it upside down.'

He was either brilliant, or having a laugh. As his mother, it was impossible to tell.

Eventually, I stopped the testing and the exercises and the relentless pressure to read. It wasn't helping. If anything, it was stripping all the enjoyment out of books for both of us. See, that's the thing — we'd always been readers, the two of us. Like many people, my journey through motherhood can be charted from A.A. Milne to J.M. Barrie to E. Nesbit to Anthony Browne. From Dr Seuss to Margaret Mahy to Roald Dahl. Books weren't books, but lands to escape to. The pushchair wasn't a pushchair, but a chariot to cart our books home from the library by the kilo. Bedtime came and went, but the stories continued long into the night.

My son's imagination came alive between the pages of those books. From the age of two till he was about four, he wore a disgusting, tatty green singlet everywhere and declared 'I'm a boy and I want never to grow up!' That phase was followed by the one where he scuttled about on his hands and knees wearing nothing but undies, insisting we call him Donkey.

If there was a prize for a vivid imagination, here was a front-runner. He turned the living room into a meadow and went on lion hunts. Together, we changed the endings of sad stories so they were completely inappropriate and ruthlessly funny. He went to sleep listening to stories on an old plastic tape deck then, like a parrot, would perform entire vignettes from memory the next morning. He became obsessed with *The Railway Children* and named his baby sister Bobbie after his favourite character, Roberta. We still call her Bobbie to this day.

Unfortunately, school reports don't grade kids on their enthusiasm for reading — just their ability. I despaired when this boy of ours who loved books so much came home with a 'not achieving' result in reading. This was in the early days of National

Standards. The simple black and white tables were layered with so much judgement. I didn't know who was failing — me or him. It was hard to control my panic, and the irrationality of my fears. What if he never learnt to read? What if he became a brilliant lawyer but had to read statutes upside down?

Mostly, though, I was just sad. Our boy stopped wearing his tatty green singlet and started walking upright. School had robbed him of a little bit of his sparkle.

Through it all, I kept reading aloud to him. By lamplight, I read the books he couldn't read himself because they were too big, the words too small, or they involved just so much effort. My parenting bible in those days was not a 'learn to read' manual or dyslexia home-test kit, but a book by Daniel Pennac called *The Rights of the Reader*.

I read it over and over again. Pennac's theory is that we push kids to read too soon. That by forcing them to read before they're ready, we strip all the enjoyment out of reading for kids.

The whole book is infinitely quotable — a must-read for anyone who has ever known the subversive pleasure of reading for its own sake. It's a book especially for parents who are struggling with the enormity of those black-and-white tables that simply do not help them understand why their kid can't, won't or doesn't want to read.

Of course, my boy did eventually learn to read. He was about eight when he sussed it out, and he didn't so much read as inhale books. He read everything he could get his hands on. I deeply suspect, though, that when he reads, he's not doing it because he loves it as much as reading to find out what happens next. Which is kind of the point, isn't it?

Now, at the age of 14, he's probably read more widely than me. He can still recite long passages of *Peter Pan* from memory.

If I give him the first lines of 'The Island' by A.A. Milne, he'll finish off the poem because he just can't help himself. He's read *The Diary of Anne Frank* so many times that when we were watching *The Chase* on TV, he answered half a dozen obscure questions about the book correctly while the rest of us looked on dumbfounded.

For all of that, he still prefers being read to. If a book is available on audio book, he'll choose that instead of the paper volume. And sometimes he doesn't read anything for weeks on end. I'm OK with that. I've come to accept that having a kid that defies labels is OK too. Ironically, we named him after the famous American author, Cormac McCarthy. He's a writer who would probably have failed National Standards too. He shuns punctuation and writes stream-of-consciousness prose that defies every rule in the book. He also won the Pulitzer Prize.

Looking back now, this period of reading struggle only lasted about two or three years. In the scheme of things, it's nothing. But like any difficult parenting phase, when you're in the thick of it, it feels like it's going to go on forever.

The important thing when teaching your kid to read is not to panic. It's simple. Line up the letters, sound them out, read. If your kid can't do it, do it for them.

No Holiday: On the decision whether to have 'another'

BY SIMON SWEETMAN

Simon Sweetman is a music journalist, short story writer and poet living in Wellington. He blogs at Off The Tracks.

I always wanted a daughter named Billie. Simple, really. As soon as I heard Billie Holiday's voice I was sold. Her voice, that sound, and the idea of her name being Billie — it all just hung in the air there for me. I wanted, nearly 100 years after Holiday's birth, for it to be my tribute. I get as close as I ever get to crying when I hear her voice. But we knew we were having a son. We had no names for boys. Besides, they all sounded like something you'd name a dog. Otis. Hugo. Rufus. Mongrel . . . We settled on Oscar. Happy with our decision, we returned home from the hospital. A week later we heard the neighbours whistle for their wee dog: 'Oscar! Oscar!'

Our Oscar's life has been a charmed one. His dad working at

home and introducing him to all the music he'll ever need, and far more. A mother who could not love him more. We know we spoil him. He's so very precious. He didn't come easy. We had, like many people, several unsuccessful attempts at getting — or rather staying — pregnant. When it looked like the baby bump that would become the baby that would become Oscar was going to make it to full term we were able, just, to remove the deer-in-headlights look and feel that realisation sweep across us both. And just as I started to feel something approaching elation I was handed a nappy and told to strap it on the tiny young lad. I had a whole new learning curve. Time to step up. My whole life's achievements up to that point had been a sports victory, a great gig and a sculling contest. The real work, and real joy, was now here.

Katy did not enjoy being pregnant. It was difficult. She had daily injections and I had to do them for her. She hates needles. You realise how in love you are and how vulnerable life is when you're sat at the end of the bed each morning, a cold needle between you being the thing that's going to help you bring life into this world. I kept thinking of that line from *The Young Ones* where Vivian is about to do 'acupuncture' on Neil by tapping a six-inch nail up his nostril to clear the flu. 'You might feel a bit of a prick,' Vivian says. 'So what's new?' is the reply. I never shared this out loud. I steadied my hand each morning and found a new place to drill, avoiding the gathering bruises.

Within days of Oscar existing, my mum suggested we 'hurry up and try again'. We were reminded that we were both 'getting on'. In the days and weeks and months, and now years, since we've had our world turned inside out and upside down — magically so, sure — we've been asked by closest friends and total strangers when we are 'gonna try again', and if we're 'hoping for one of each', as if the set needs to be collected; as if you've done it right to get both boy and girl, as if there are just two types in the world.

Miscarriage is brutal. Our second seemed particularly cruel — we were a day off the 12-week scan. The first had been no picnic, either. I was at work; we had friends staying who, at that point, didn't know our near-news. They were left to, well, mop up. Being good friends, we were in good hands. You finally meet the drop-everything-for-you type of friends you hope you've got in these situations.

I guess that first experience — me not being there, cursing a fucking weekend shift in a dead-end retail job — is really what made me so fiercely protective of our pregnancy with Oscar. And of the one that didn't work ahead of Oscar. I didn't abstain from drinking. I did enjoy the comforts of a live-in sober driver. But I was alert to it all. Always on. Ever fearful, always hopeful. We were going to do this.

And we did.

People told Katy she was glowing. And I winced. I felt her worry. People told us it was a walk in the park and I sat baffled. It hadn't really been that at all.

Discussions around children and having families are so often so gross, I guess because we take it for granted. So many of us really don't know how lucky we are.

Well, here we were now. Runs on the board . . . finally!

And then the questions again, and again, of why we were 'leaving it so late' and how 'we better get a move on' and 'didn't we want one of each' and weren't we 'hoping for more' and wasn't the aim to 'have another'?

A boy and a girl would be lovely, sure. I am a boy. Katy is a girl. It's understandable to want to make something in your own image, to see your own image in someone else. Two boys would be just great too, perhaps. He'd have a friend. A little brother. Someone to teach the dance moves to.

But there is so much wrapped up in it all. And every experience is different. We celebrated our 10-year wedding anniversary and a family member told us that 'we hadn't done very well', meaning just one child was not good enough. As if that was the real and only reason for any marriage. As if staying together and channelling each other's strengths and covering for each other's weaknesses, or just knowing them and still being in love with each other, wasn't enough of a win after 10 years. As if a funny, kooky, quirky kid that's healthy and happy and knows all the words to Phil Collins's 'In The Air Tonight' wasn't enough of a win after 10 years.

We fended off a few more reminders that time was marching on. As if we didn't have our own mirrors. Or markers. Or marks . . .

But we never really talked about whether we'd be having 'another'. Because in the running of the house and the quest for work and happiness — or one, or the other — we just kept the machine going. Found our groove, found what worked. I'm better at home. Katy is better at work. That's how it is for us. Everyone finds their groove. It's slightly different, or very different, for everyone.

Just as the decision around having children — any or how many — is different for everyone.

We finally found a chance to talk about it after the most unsubtle hints in the world. My mum's latest pressing concern was to know when she could start putting 'all the old strollers' on TradeMe.

Oscar will be an only child. He won't be a lonely child. That's my hope. He already has friends. And family. And he's the type of kid who bounds into Mickey Mouse's house at Disneyland

and shouts, 'Yo Mickey, what's cookin'?' or dances in Cuba Mall with the wandering Hare Krishna singing folk. So he'll be OK. I reckon.

Does it break my heart a little when he says, 'But I wish that I could have a brother'? Yes, it does.

Do I wish we were having another child? Yes. Yes, I do.

The spirit of Billie sings somewhere in my heart.

We've made the right decision. And there are lots of factors in that — nothing is ever easy. But it is right, because it's the best fit for us. It was never anyone else's decision. That doesn't make it easier. Even knowing that doesn't exactly help.

Did I imagine having 'another', having 'one of each', 'completing the set'? Sure. Of course. But we've made a great family. We love each other. We're working on doing the best we can.

A whole good day: When parenting finally feels like you thought it would

BY HOLLY WALKER

Holly Walker lives in Wellington and works as a children's advocate. She served in Parliament as a Green MP, and her first book, The Whole Intimate Mess, *was published in 2017.*

On the day my daughter turned three, a man gave me a chopping board. It was a lovely chopping board, made from caramel-coloured blocks of recycled rimu that had been glued together and clamped in a vice. The man had made it himself. He brought it over to my house in the afternoon, along with a miniature Pinky bar for my daughter, Esther.

I met this man about five years ago, when I was first running for Parliament. He was the chair of the local peace group, and hosted a debate for the candidates. Later he became a dedicated campaign volunteer. He was kind and generous, and donated several of his chopping boards to fundraising auctions. After I left Parliament, earlier than I had planned, he asked if he could gift me one as a token of support and appreciation. It took me almost three years to follow up and accept his offer.

It wasn't that I didn't want it, though we did have three other chopping boards already. Two were wedding presents, building blocks of our joint kitchen. One was a birthday gift from my stepfather about two years ago. That one was made from a slice of fallen pohutukawa tree blown over in the wind on Great Barrier Island. We used to be good at taking care of them, oiling them regularly along with our cast-iron pans, but slowly we fell out of the habit.

After Esther was born and I left Parliament, things were hard. I was having trouble with anxiety, and my partner was suffering from chronic pain. Maintaining our possessions, and even making a time to receive a gift from a kind supporter, were low on the list of priorities.

We took the same approach to most of our responsibilities, apart from keeping ourselves and Esther clean and fed, and showing up in the places we needed to be. That was enough — often it felt like too much.

Our front fence, which is a retaining wall, is sagging and cracking. Each time there's an earthquake in Wellington, it cracks a little more. In a big one recently, a cinder block fell clean out.

There is a 1976 Austin Mini Clubman slowly rusting in a neighbour's garage across the road. We bought it in the summer after I was elected to Parliament, with visions of me becoming 'that MP lady with the little green car'. We drove it back from Kaiapoi while I memorised my maiden speech in the passenger seat. We meant to sell it three years ago, but we can't seem to do it. Every three months we renew the registration, resigned.

Our house is called the Herb Cottage. The woman who lived

there before us was a herbalist who operated a massage studio out the back. It smelled of lavender and calendula when we moved in. We knew she wanted someone to buy it who would take care of her herbs, so we wrote her a letter to that effect to accompany our offer. She accepted.

Three years later, the garden runs wild. Fennel taller than us chokes the apple tree, nasturtiums spread across the lawn from every planter bed, and the garden seat her husband built has rotted and collapsed.

Inside the house, paper and books are piled on every surface. Esther's odd socks are sprinkled through the house like seasoning. The cat luxuriates in piles of clean, unfolded washing. Sometimes I feel like we exist on the surface of our life. We get through each day, eat, run the dishwasher and collapse into bed to do it all again. Dealing with longer-term projects seems impossible, overwhelming. So we don't. Most of the time I no longer feel guilty about this, recognising that survival is our primary aim. Most of the time I'm OK with that. But it's hard.

The other day was a good day. A whole good day, from start to finish. All three of us woke refreshed. Dave cooked us a breakfast of mushrooms on toast. The sun was shining. We had a family outing to the new playground at Avalon Park. Dave slept in the warm sun while Esther and I explored. She was in her element: brave, adventurous, independent. We stayed for two and a half hours. I wish I could live here, she said to me as we left — but she left without complaint.

We went to a café for lunch. She was dehydrated and hungry after her morning of playing in the sun, but she lasted. We came home. She didn't fall asleep on the way. We watched a movie — *Inside Out* — to get through the post-lunch lull. She didn't fall asleep then either. I painted her nails. She didn't really get the movie, but she watched it anyway. 'When I'm five I will know how to watch it,' she said. I cried, especially at the bit when Joy realises that she needs Sadness with her. That you can't have one without the other.

Then Esther helped me make dinner. She had her own pan and little bits of each thing I was cooking, and she stirred and chatted away. The meal was ready early, and she ate it. Every last bit. Then she had a bath, read a story with Dave, a story with me. I turned out the light, sang her 'Pokarekare Ana', and she was out.

It was a day just like I thought every day as a parent would be, but which so few are. A day in which Dave and I were both present, and relaxed. A day in which Esther had fun, and all her needs were met. In which we rested, ate well and took care of each other.

After dinner I drank a glass of wine and oiled the chopping boards, all four of them. They came up just fine.

My son is turning five tomorrow

BY EMILY WRITES

My son is turning five tomorrow. I can't quite fathom this, since it feels like yesterday I was pacing the living room, my cell phone on my shoulder, telling a Plunket nurse, 'Please, he won't stop crying and I don't know what to do!'

Every day felt like forever. Every day felt like an ordeal of trying to learn to parent while also trying to work out why he was so ill. And now, suddenly, he's hip-high and telling me that 'Red blood cells carry oxygen around the body, Mama.'

Discussing his birthday has been a three-month ordeal of him steadfastly refusing to have any type of birthday that isn't an 'Eric Yum Pry Mews' birthday. Since seeing the Olympics he has been obsessed with newsreader Eric Young from *Prime News*. He thinks his full name is Eric Yum Pry Mews. He talks to him through the television.

So here we are. Tomorrow he will have an Eric Young *Prime News* party. Because, well, why not? He loves Eric Young because Eric Young is the Olympics and also 'he does important mews every night, Mama. Even when you're tired, Eric Yum Pry Mews still does that mews', and you can't argue with that, can you?

But last night I had a dream that Eric Young sprang out of an Eric Young cake. He was dressed in his *Prime News* suit wearing his signature black-rim glasses. All around me children were dressed as tiny Eric Youngs.

'Ka kite ano and goodnight,' they all said in monotone, over and over again.

Are my fears about my baby boy growing up manifesting into nightmares about New Zealand television's most elegant and classy newsreader?

Birthdays are a celebration, especially for children. My son talks about growing up 'a size'. He says, 'When I am a size bigger, I will still be your baby.' He tells me when he sees my brow furrow that 'Did you know, Mama, did you know that Daddy is so tall as the ceiling but Nana still call him her baby boy, Mama. Did you know that?'

Maybe he can see a part of me I thought I wasn't showing. Even when they're small we send them out into the world, and we hope in our absence every other adult will protect them. We hope they'll come back to us. Can he see that worry behind my pride?

I remember lying with him when he was brand new. My aching body curled around him. I couldn't take my eyes off him. I couldn't believe he was mine. That feeling has never gone away. I often catch myself looking at him the same way and thinking — is this all a dream?

He is everything I could have hoped for in a child. Generous and kind and a friend to all. He has all of the qualities I don't. All of the best qualities of his father. For so long, when he was very sick as a baby, we just hoped he'd make it. There wasn't room for any other wishes in that murky well.

And here we are. He outshines even our greatest hopes for him.

He has nightmares sometimes. Before bed we lie down together and I give him three dreams to choose from:

'You and Isaac own a cake shop. Isaac makes pancakes shaped like hearts and you make donuts with pink frosting. Annie and Ronnie are your taste testers.'

'You and Billie are astronauts and you live on Mars. You dance around Saturn's rings and you play hopscotch on the moon.'

'You and Daddy drive diggers. You make the roads shiny and new so all of the cars can drive down them.'

He picks his favourite dream and I whisper in his ear a made-up magic to ensure there's no nightmares.

He is five. He can write his name, but more importantly he can put his arm around another child and say, 'Hey, are you OK, friend?'

When he was a baby I thought I'd never get him out of my bed. Once in a blue moon now he climbs in next to me and I try not to squeeze him too tight — I never thought I'd be so happy to be sharing a bed with both of my babies again.

He will soon be too old for whispered magic but I'm going to savour these days. They did fly by so fast, but I had the best co-pilot, so I feel like we enjoyed the view along the way.

I used to worry — is he sleeping enough? Eating enough? Now my worries are different — will he be OK at school? Will other kids be kind? Maybe worry is a constant friend to mothers. But I know too that my worries pale in comparison to the worries of others. And that alone quietens the voice of fear and encourages me to reach out to him.

Five isn't always a promise. When you have a sick child you know this.

My baby — always baby — will be five tomorrow. He'll wear the suit we bought him to look like Eric Yum Pry Mews.

He will be his usual self, but five. Quirky and kind. Silly and funny and generous. Sunshine on our rainiest day. Better than we could have ever imagined.

If you're starting your odyssey now, holding your brand-new baby, know this: this is the greatest adventure. The most wonderous voyage. The hardest but best journey.

You think you can't love them more than you do now? Oh, the capacity of our hearts for our children!

I could burst.

My gracious plenty. My baby is five.

How lucky, lucky, lucky we are.

Acknowledgements

It seems a strange thing to kick off acknowledgements in a book by thanking a power company — but The Spinoff Parents (https://thespinoff.co.nz/category/parenting/) and many of the words in this book wouldn't exist without Flick Electric. Thank you to all of the staff at Flick who have chosen year after year to support writing in New Zealand by funding the Parents section on The Spinoff website.

Thank you to Duncan for inviting me to edit the Parents section of The Spinoff and for having faith in my ability to be an editor even when I didn't have faith myself. Thank you Catherine for your patience with me and for teaching me so much. Thank you Toby for your kindness and for letting me cry on your shoulder. Thank you to all of the staff at the good ship Spinoff for your support.

Thank you to the wonderful writers included in this book. I am so grateful you have chosen to share your writing with the world through this collection. It's a very brave thing to do and I firmly believe it honours and builds the type of strong and generous parenting community we all want. It has been such a pleasure working with you.

Thank you to everyone who has ever written anything for The Spinoff Parents and everyone who has ever read anything on The Spinoff Parents. Thank you for making this dream come true.

Thank you Margaret for always believing in me. Thank you for urging me on when it all seemed too hard. I know the relationship between a writer and their publisher is a very special thing — I think I'm the world's luckiest writer to have you. Thank you Stuart, this book just would not have come together without you. Thank you to everyone at Penguin Random House — your support, especially at the beginning of the year, meant the world to me.

To the CBC crew — thank you for everything, I don't know what I'd do without you babes. To Jean — thank you for Fridays. To Caroline — I love you and I'm so glad we are friends. To Chris and Gem — I can't wait till we are all old and our husbands are dead and we get to live on a commune together.

Thank you to my husband. Nothing happens without you. You are the love of my life and I pinch myself every day knowing I get to spend forever with someone who is so wonderful and just super outrageously hot. You're an absolute DILF and you know full well I'd be a fucking mess without you. God I love you so much it's stupid.

Thank you to my baby boys — I hope you will be proud of me. Everything I do is for you. You're the best thing that ever happened to me. I love you 24 and Twinkle too.

Finally, thank you to my sister Jo. You are everything to me. You are the kindest, most generous, most loving person I have ever known. You inspire me to be the best mum I can be. This book is for you.

Popular blogger Emily Writes gives words of encouragement to sleep-deprived parents everywhere.

With two small boys, both non-sleepers, Emily finds herself awake in the wee small hours night after night. Her writing is frequently done then, and she offers her own often hilarious and always heart-warming experiences to other exhausted parents. She describes the frustrations as well as the tender moments of real parenting, as opposed to what you thought it was going to be like, or what well-meaning advice-givers tell you it *should* be like.

A must-have for all new parents and parents-to-be.